Keeping Up with *the* Joneses

The Extraordinary Journey of a Very Ordinary Couple

Karen Fitzgerald Jones

Karen Jones is an outstanding writer and story-teller. This story is the real life story of her marriage to her late husband, Rev. Bill Jones. It's a story of passion and pain as their five decades of marriage display the realities of "in sickness and in health, for better, for worse, till death do us part." The honesty in this story is refreshing and gives permission to all of us to live to the fullest with the promise of "faith, hope, and love."

Dr. Doug Beacham
General Superintendent
International Pentecostal Holiness Church

Keeping Up with the Joneses is an invitation—join the trip, enter the story.

Karen Jones tells the truth about life as it is lived: love and laughter, disappointment and hope, calling and loss. Through her life with Bill—his ministry, his long journey through illness, and her life after his death—we are reminded that ordinary lives, faithfully lived with Jesus, become extraordinary testimonies of grace.

These pages feel personal because they are. Karen's story gives voice to our own questions, our own pain, and our own perseverance. As we read Bill's words and hear his voice, we are drawn into a narrative shaped by love, endurance, and trust in God through every season.

This is a book to enter slowly, to feel deeply, and to carry with you—long after the final page.

Chris Maxwell
Author, Pastor

Growing up with Bill Jones as my pastor has been a tremendous blessing to my life and ministry. *Keeping Up with the Joneses* has given me greater insight into this wonderful man and his family. It has given me a fuller revelation and a greater appreciation for their story.

In these pages you will find an engaging story of love that will bring bursts of laughter and tears. This is a rare look behind the curtain of a minister's personal, professional, and family life that most do not get to see. Real people with real struggles and real victories. Many will relate to the young romance and the early excitement of marriage. Some will find a bond in reading stories about relational perseverance. All this speaks of God's abundant provision in the life of the faithful. Pastor Bill often said, "There are no throwaway people." This sentiment will live on with me.

This book was an emotional journey for me, and you will not be able to put it away either.

Pastor John Case
Celebration Outreach Center
Elberton, Georgia

Karen Fitzgerald Jones opens a window into her life with her husband William Jones and their sons, Blake and Yubo. The book provided me the opportunity to laugh out loud, to experience their joys, to read about their trials, and to simply grieve.

The multiple miracles recorded in this book allow an opportunity to share in the wonder of God's power in preparing and delivering those awe-inspiring events. The book is raw, honest, and transparent. Easy-to-read and straightforward, this book permits the reader to feel the emotions outlined on the pages.

The author, Karen Fitzgerald Jones, was my middle school teacher. We clicked right away as we each shared a strong, independent spirit, a love for reading, and a love for God. Reading her book was a surreal experience for me. Karen always will remain the best teacher and a positive influencer in my life. She is an obedient servant to God, which includes writing and sharing this book. While it honors the journey of the Jones family members, particularly her husband William "Billy" Jones, this book allows the reader an opportunity to witness their love story and God's love. Readers will find the transparency refreshing. Plan to be profoundly blessed and moved!

Dr. Andrea D. Daniel
President, Athens Technical College
***Georgia Trend's* Most Influential 500 Leaders of Georgia-2025**

Contents

Foreword

It looked like a spotlight was over her head. Then I saw it....

The ceiling of the church opened, and a baby fell out of a sheet, onto a sheet, and landed in the lady's arms. It was so real I thought perhaps the entire congregation had seen the vision.

I called her to the front of the church and told her what I'd seen. I didn't know until later that she was the Pastor's wife, Karen Jones. I only knew what I had witnessed in the vision.

Fast-forward five years. We were ministering in a revival in San Jose, California, and I was drawn to a beautiful pregnant girl from Heritage Home for Unwed Mothers. Immediately, I was back in the church sanctuary in Georgia, and -again- I saw the wonder of the baby falling from the sky. Somehow, I knew this young girl was the mother of the baby in my vision.

I hadn't spoken to Bill and Karen Jones for five years. I wasn't even certain where they lived, so it took some digging to find them.

How do you ask someone, "Do you want to have a baby?"

It took a series of miracles of biblical proportions for the promised child, Blake, to fall into the arms of Bill and Karen. I was there; I witnessed it.

But they are no strangers to a rollercoaster life of both challenges and miracles. They demonstrate how to navigate the whirlwinds of the unpredictable journey.

Karen Jones has so bravely lifted the veil of Bill and her story, and aren't we readers glad for her honesty? You will laugh and cry as you experience the adventures of two lives well lived.

Grab yourself a cup of tea, prop up your feet, and get ready to enjoy, ***Keeping Up with the Joneses***.

Reba Rambo
Grammy and Dove Award winning
Christian Singer and Songwriter

Prologue

Karen's Yearbook Message to Bill: May 24, 1974

> ***Our life will be happy and meaningful — we'll keep it that way. Who knows (except God) what our future holds in store for us. Happiness, sorrow, great things, and tragedy. But God will help us, and we'll lean on each other.***

Bill's Yearbook Message to Karen: May 24, 1974

> ***I am so glad God worked out all of the tricky problems He had to get us here. We will keep Him first, and He will keep us first. I look forward to our future life with the utmost optimism and enthusiasm! You are wonderful, and you are mine alone!***

These wise words came from my daddy.

> ***"Honey, EVERYONE has a story."***

I know he's right, but our story is different by anyone's standards. It's a story that needs to be told, and it seems that I am the one to tell it. I think Bill would want it that way. He often said that we should write a book, especially after I retired and had more free time. Somehow ***LIFE*** got in the way, and I am just now getting around to it. The inspiration behind this book is stronger now; the need to write it is more pressing.

I promise to be honest, and I will not sugarcoat. My tendency has always been to be straight up with folks, and Bill encouraged me to do that.

> ***"Don't backpedal, Babe! Tell it like it is."***

So, I will.

This is a love story, but it's not a fairy tale. I believe you will laugh with us and cry with us. I want you to see the miracles — *not* simply coincidences — that touched our lives and changed us. My prayer is that **YOU** will be inspired and changed through the reading of this book. Some of our story is sentimental, but much of it is raw. All of it has been lived in the shadow of ministry. Our hearts were always centered on serving Jesus, but we were not perfect people, and our story will show that.

I'm going to share bits and pieces of our love letters throughout the book. We kept them all — two boxes full! The excerpts from our letters are presented —pretty much— as we wrote them. I will occasionally correct some (not all) grammar or spelling, but the content will be authentic. We were only eighteen years old when these letters were written; they are very unpolished, but so were we. I am choosing to share with you our very personal letters so that you can truly see what was in our hearts. I also have some cards and Facebook posts which I will share from more recent years.

Many years have passed, but the conversations we had with each other and with friends have remained vivid in my memory. I have shared bits and pieces of our journey in small groups and larger conferences over and over throughout the years. The quotes that are given may not be word-for-word, but they are accurate in content.

Regardless of the book's title, I am ***NOT*** asking you to "Keep Up with the Joneses." Just grab a soda or a cup of coffee; get comfortable in your favorite chair, and ***join*** us on a trip through **OUR** story. Hold onto your seats, and buckle up; it will be a wild ride! I promise that you won't get bored, and I believe you will be blessed by taking this journey with us.

-Karen

Chapter One

Who Are We?

Bill: Facebook Post June 15, 2022

Happy Anniversary to my wife of now forty-eight years. Karen Jones, you are a wonder. Who else would love me like you do? Our life is an adventure of love and a testimony of grace. I sure am proud to call you, my wife.

Before we start this journey together, you need to know a little about who we are. Well, sorry to disappoint you; we are NOT famous. Bill was not a professional wrestler with the WWE even though he was built for it. My daddy once teased him and said that he would be his manager; he even had a "professional" name for Bill — SCARBELLY! You will understand THAT better later on in the book. I sing a bit, but I've never had a professional recording. I sang a couple of times on local television stations, but I doubt that you ever saw one of those programs. This book is about two very ordinary people who happened to live an extraordinary life together. I love that Bill called it "an adventure of love and a testimony of grace." He nailed it! *The Joneses* — could we be any more ORDINARY than that? You be the judge.

Bill

Bill Jones was born in a hurricane! He was born five days before Hurricane Hazel hit eastern North Carolina in October 1954. The family often relayed the story of how baby Billy had been placed in a crib in his parents' bedroom in Clinton, North Carolina. The storm was raging outside, so someone went to bring the newborn into the middle room of the house with the rest of the family. Mere seconds after he was picked up out of the crib, a piece of sheet metal came flying through the bedroom window shattering glass into the crib. Bill's life was spared for the FIRST time at the tender age of five days old. It would not be the LAST time that supernatural intervention saved his life.

Young Billy

Bill was the son of Henry Floyd Jones and Pinkie Blake Medford Jones. He grew up in a modest frame house, the youngest of five children. His mom thought she was either starting menopause or had become very ill when she became pregnant at the age of 40. She was 41 when little Billy made his entrance into this world. The realization that his parents were much older than the parents of his friends scared Billy when he was in elementary school. He often prayed that God would keep his mama alive until he was grown and on his own. God honored the prayer of that little boy.

The Joneses had a solid history of ministry and serving Jesus. Pinkie's father, N.J. (Noyel John) Medford, was a respected pastor in eastern North Carolina. Pinkie was actually named after a pioneer female evangelist from Georgia named Pinkie Blake. Little Billy heard many stories about his grandfather's struggles to support his young family on his ministry income, and those stories caused him to resist the calling of God on his own life for a few years. His paternal grandfather, William Bryant Jones, was a faithful deacon and church leader. Baby Billy was named after both of these godly men, and their spiritual mantles were certainly evident on him in later years.

Pinkie: Letter to Bill: January 9, 1973

When you were a baby, I felt and have since that the Lord had a special work for you to do. I am glad that you (are) letting the Lord lead and hope you will always stay committed to Him and

> ***that He will use you to win many souls for Him. I am and will be praying for you. I named you for both of your grandads hoping you would sing like your grandad Jones and preach like your grandad Medford. I am praying that the Lord will help you to do both — sing and preach — and use you like He wants to.***

Pinkie had no idea how God would answer her prayer on both counts. His Grandaddy Medford was a big man, and Bill Jones inherited his size as well as his powerful voice.

His family attended the local Pentecostal Holiness Church in Clinton. It was a solid congregation filled with dedicated and faithful parishioners. Bill told me so many stories about some of the church members; I felt as if I knew each one. He attended Sunday School, youth meetings, Bible schools, and campmeeting services in the summer. He also considered attending Emmanuel College in Georgia (a denominational college), but the North Carolina colleges also piqued his interest. Bill was intelligent; he worked hard and made good grades. He also played football because he was a BIG guy! Bill was responsible, likeable, and kind. He was always a trustworthy friend.

Young Floyd & Pinkie

Bill's dad, Floyd, would take the family to Topsail Island when Bill was young. They would sleep in a beach buggy his dad had made. Floyd was a mechanic for a while; he could tinker with just about anything. By the time I met him, he was running a small greenhouse operation and providing plants to local businesses. Bill considered going into horticulture at one time and expanding the business, but God had other plans. He also thought about studying marine biology because he enjoyed the ocean so much. Since he was an excellent student, he knew that he could pursue many different career options.

Older Floyd & Pinkie

High School Senior

Bill applied to Emmanuel College, but he kept options open in case he decided to stay in North Carolina. At the time, Emmanuel was a junior college, so he finally decided to go to Georgia for the first two years and then transfer back to North Carolina to finish his degree. When Bill Jones made up his mind, there was NO STOPPING him! God already knew that, but GOD was going to change Bill's mind once He got him to Georgia!

Karen

I was born, Karen Leigh Fitzgerald, in the Shenandoah Valley of Virginia. I have always called myself a hillbilly, but my daddy corrects me.

Young Karen

"Girl, you were born in the valley!"

I still think I'm a hillbilly, and I'm proud to be one. Natural Bridge, Virginia, is one of the most beautiful places in America. I grew up looking at the stunningly beautiful Blue Ridge Mountains every day of my life! The changing seasons, the sunshine and shadows, the misty mornings, the snow-covered mountaintops, and the glorious colors of autumn were on a regular playlist for me.

Karen, Barry, and Sandy

I am a first-born child; I had a younger sister, Sandy (now in Heaven), and a baby brother, Barry. My parents, Cole and Dorothy Fitzgerald, were only eighteen years old when I was born. Bill's parents were about the same age as my grandparents. Most of my family members are hard-working folks. They are also quite intelligent and creative, but many did not have the money or the opportunity to go to college. Some didn't graduate high school. My mama passed the test for her GED, and my daddy took classes and earned his high school diploma while he was out of work for nearly a year due to a serious injury he sustained at his factory. He had three children at the time, and he knew he needed to make changes in order to provide for his family. Daddy always encouraged all three of us to take education seriously and to work hard. He raised us to be independent, and he succeeded at that task.

Young Cole & Dorothy

My parents were two of the hardest-working people I've ever known. Mama never sat down! She worked from before daylight until everyone else had gone to bed. She never met a problem she couldn't solve, and she could do just about anything! She cut our hair; she made our clothes; she was a talented artist and always worked outside the home to help with the finances. My mom has gone to Heaven, but Daddy is still splitting wood, cutting cedars, and cleaning his gutters at eighty-nine years of age! He also has a great sense of humor and loves a good practical joke more than anyone I know! I come from GOOD stock!

I grew up in the Natural Bridge Pentecostal Holiness Church. My church was a country church; Bill's was more of a "town" church. We did grow up singing out of the same hymnal, studying the same Sunday School literature, and hearing some of the same evangelists during church revival meetings. We both grew up knowing what it was like to be misunderstood and ridiculed because of our religious beliefs. We shared a history before we even met which helped to create a strong bond early on.

Older Cole & Dorothy

When I was fourteen years old, I fell in love, and it wasn't with Bill. I didn't even know him yet. I gave my heart to a young man one grade ahead of me in school. We were so young, but we became quite serious early on. Serious enough that my parents were concerned. They knew I wanted to go to college and be a teacher. They also knew the risks associated with young love, and they didn't want me to make a mistake and destroy my dreams.

Karen 10th grade

God intervened in an unusual way when I went to church camp in Dublin, Virginia. I had attended camp for several summers and thoroughly loved it! This would be my last summer camp because I was getting ready to start my first real job. God touched me during one of the nightly services, and I poured my heart out to Him. I had given my heart to Jesus in my primary Sunday School class, but I cried out to God that night at the altar and surrendered my future to Him. I submitted my wants and dreams to Him and sincerely asked for His guidance in my life.

I didn't hear God's *audible* voice, but I definitely FELT it!

End it. End it now.

There was no doubt in my mind what He meant. I needed to end the relationship with my first love. My heart broke at that moment; I cried and cried because I loved that boy. I knew he loved me, and I knew how hurt he would be. I have never been as sure of anything as I was sure that God was giving me a directive, but it was a heartbreaking command.

Sometimes, God asks us to do difficult things. Our parents do that as well. They know what's best, and they ask us to do the hard things for our own good. Let me say here that I never stopped loving that boy. Bill knew all about him; I did not hide that part of my life from him. I also know that my life with my first love would have been a very different life from the one I shared with Bill. I believe Bill made me a better woman in many ways. Several years ago, I found out that my first love was fighting serious cancer. My heart hurt for him, and I prayed for his healing. When my mother called to tell me that he had passed away, I cried in my car. Please understand that *true* love never dies. I may have loved him, but I was ***not*** meant to marry him. *Falling in love with someone does not necessarily make him or her the right person for you.* That is a truth we all need to grasp.

I ended the relationship after I returned home from camp. I cried; he cried, and even my mother cried. No one understood why I was breaking up with him. I didn't understand it myself except that I knew what God had said. It would take a couple of years before I saw the "WHY." I have thanked God many times for how He spoke to me that night at the altar in Dublin. It changed the trajectory of my life in all the right ways.

I definitely wanted to attend Emmanuel College in Franklin Springs, Georgia. I wanted desperately to sing in the college choir. That was my main reason for attending; it was one of my high school dreams! I have never considered myself to be exceptionally bright, but I studied hard and worked hard. I made good grades and was given an opportunity to take one class in summer school and skip the eleventh grade. I didn't have to think very long about that decision! Math was always the most difficult subject for me, but a few weeks of ONE class versus nine months of SIX classes was a fairly easy problem to solve! UMMMMMMM…. let's go for the summer school option! I was able to graduate high school in 1972, the SAME year Bill graduated in North Carolina.

I had surrendered my future to God at the altar in Dublin. God had a plan for Bill and for me, and He was putting it into motion without either of us having a clue! I was accepted at Emmanuel and was eager to start a new chapter in my life. Little did I know what God had in store for me in Georgia!

Chapter Two

Georgia On My Mind

In September of 1972, Mama and Daddy helped me load up our car like the Beverly Hillbillies, and we hit the road for Franklin Springs, Georgia! Franklin Springs is a small town about thirty miles from Athens, home of the University of Georgia. Go DAWGS! Leaving home for college at the tender age of seventeen was quite the thrill! My parents were a bit concerned with me being so far away from home, but a small Christian school seemed a good fit for me. I had visited the college during high school, and I knew that it was where I wanted to be.

I was accustomed to hot summer days in Virginia, but I had never encountered heat and humidity like September days in Georgia! Have mercy! It was HOT. I don't perspire; I sweat like a man working on hot asphalt! It isn't pretty, and that's all I'm going to say about that. I had long hair in the fall of 1972, and it had never been frizzy... until GEORGIA! Our dorm was not air-conditioned either, and it didn't take very many weeks before I trimmed a good chunk off with no regrets.

One of my best friends from my hometown also came to Emmanuel with her parents that September. Paula Price had been my friend since we were four years old. We went to the same schools and the same little church. We attended church camps together as well, so it was not a surprise that we would go to the same college. Paula was a year ahead of me in school, but when I skipped my junior year and graduated in 1972, it meant that

Paula and Karen at youth camp

we could also start college together. In order to make new friends, we decided not to room together as freshmen. It was a good decision, but we did room together our sophomore year which was great fun. By that time, we were both in love with "Billys" from North Carolina and had LOTS to talk about and plans to make! You'll learn more about Paula in a later chapter.

Getting adjusted to college life was wonderful! I loved it! Making new friends, registering for classes, and beginning my first job in the college work-study program were all exciting for me. My parents could not help me with my college expenses, so the work-study program was essential to supplement the scholarships I had received and the student loans I had taken. My first job was in the admissions office which was great because I learned many of the names of the incoming freshmen. Emmanuel was only a two-year junior college at the time, and I think the enrollment was around 500 or so. Today, it is Emmanuel University with a much larger student body. The campus is absolutely gorgeous, and I am thankful for my experiences there. The dorms are also air-conditioned now, by the way! Praise God!

One day I was working with a new friend in admissions, and we were going through some student data cards. We found a card with the name, William Noyel Jones. She looked at me, and I looked at her.

We both said, ***"No-YELL?" What kind of name is that?"***

Little did I know that I would spend the next fifty-three years of my life finding out what "kind of name" that was and the man who was attached to it.

Just for clarification, the "y" is silent; it is pronounced "Noel."

The admissions office also had a big window that looked out over one of the college walkways. As we worked, my friends and I (all girls) would take every chance we could to check out the college boys walking back and forth to the gym or the cafeteria. What fun we had! We each took turns claiming which guy we wanted to get to know better. I saw one or two that caught my eye, but my first encounter with Bill didn't come until a week or so later, and it was not what you would expect.

One of the placement exams we took was an English exam. If we scored high enough, we could exempt English 101 and take an honors level English class. I had no expectations going into the test, and I was thrilled when they notified me that I was going into the honors group. I believe there were only eight or nine of us who exempted the 101 class. The professor, who is now a dear friend of mine, met with us early in the morning, one day a week. He would discuss a topic with us, give us an assignment related to that topic, and we would not meet until the next week. None of us really enjoyed having an early morning class, but it was fun to be given that type of freedom. It was a new experience for most of us.

The first day that the honors class met, I was sitting beside one of my new friends, Betty. The professor sat at the head of a table with the students sitting down the sides. Betty got my attention and glanced at one of the boys sitting across from us. He had big shoulders — football big — and a round face. His thick black hair was sticking up like he hadn't combed it, and there may have been sleep in his eyes. He obviously had just rolled out of bed and run to class. We girls had gotten up early, showered, washed our hair, and put on a little make-up! Back in those days, that's what we did. She giggled, and so did I. His appearance just struck us as really funny, especially that early in the morning! Guess what? That was William ***NoYELL*** Jones, and one day, I would marry him. What is also interesting is that a couple of years later when Betty met Mike -the love of her life- Bill performed their wedding ceremony! Don't tell me that God doesn't have a sense of humor!

We had mutual friends that first college quarter also, so we got to know each other but only as acquaintances. Bill showed no special interest in me, and —during the early weeks of that quarter— my attention was directed elsewhere. Neither of us had any romantic plans that included each other. God had a plan, though, but He had to do some creative maneuvering in both of our hearts to get us on the same track. Initially, we both resisted God's plan, especially Bill! Thankfully, God didn't give up on us!

Chapter Three

God's Plan

Paula and I already knew several fellow students because we had attended youth camp with them over the years. I had been dating a boy from Virginia who also came to Emmanuel in 1972. He was a good Christian, and we enjoyed each other's company, but it became pretty obvious within a few weeks that we were not in love. He actually broke up with me! Can you imagine that? He was the ONLY boyfriend to ever break up with ME! How dare he! I am smiling as I write this because he's a wonderful man with a beautiful and sweet wife, and I love both of them. I was angry with him at the time, but when I look back and see what God did in both of our lives, all I can do is be thankful.

After the break-up, I was free to scope out the territory and check out the other college guys which I began to do. I never went through the "icky" stage where boyfriends were concerned. I had a boyfriend in the first grade, and we are still friends to this day! He also has a beautiful wife and family. There were two or three other college students who caught my eye, but nothing developed except friendships. As the weeks went on in that first quarter, I got to know Bill Jones much better. He was funny and smart. He was also kind and loved the Lord. One thing that really mattered to me was that he was NOT planning to be a preacher. I had ***NEVER*** wanted to be a preacher's wife.

Emmanuel was in the process of developing a strong ministerial studies program, but most of the student body were planning to get an associate's degree in general education. Bill and I both planned to spend two years at Emmanuel and then transfer to a larger college or university for the last two years of our undergraduate work. I had written home and told my parents that the ministerial students were so BOLD in their search for wives! I explained how they would come up and introduce themselves.

"Hi, my name is _____. What's your name? Do you play the PIANO?"

My sweet daddy responded with ***"LIE TO THEM!!! Say NO!"***

I don't really think they were quite that transparent in their search for wives, but it felt that way to me! I did play the piano, but Daddy didn't want me to marry a preacher either. Don't get me wrong; I wanted to marry a good Christian man, but I wanted to marry the one who had a great career and could donate money for the new fellowship hall! I did not want to live in a parsonage and always be like June Cleaver! I didn't want to always keep my house clean and be so prim and proper! That's the image I had of a pastor's wife, and I wanted no part of THAT!

Bill had told me in one of our classes together that he was interested in studying marine biology or perhaps horticulture. He loved the ocean and was interested in doing something like that or turning his dad's small greenhouse operation into a large and more profitable one. Bill loved the Lord and had a strong witness which touched my heart. I began to see this big guy with the dimples and thick black hair in a new light. By the time we were preparing to leave for Christmas break, I was beginning to have deeper feelings for him which took me by surprise.

Bill was not my type, or at least that's what I told myself. I had never been attracted to a guy that large. I tended to like track stars or basketball players rather than the football types. I'm not sure why, but that's how it was. Bill had a 52-inch chest with 36-inch arms! His head was large, and his face was round. He did have the cutest dimples you ever saw and a ready smile! As my feelings for him began to change, I noticed his beautiful skin. He tanned easily while I am as white as a ghost! A friend recently described Bill as being "lumberjack" in size which is a great description. He could have been intimidating, but his pleasant and outgoing personality always seemed to put people at ease. He was easy to like and easy to be around, and I found myself wanting to be around him more and more.

Bill as EC Freshman

The problem was that Bill did NOT feel the same way about me.

One afternoon Bill mentioned that he "might" hang out in the gym that night and play some ball with other students. That's all it took for me to convince Paula to hang out in the gym with me that night! My plan was to get Bill to "notice" me. Of course, Paula knew that I was falling for Bill, and she wanted to help me out. Well, he did not show up, so Paula and I started teasing another guy and in a failed attempt to scare him, I ended up hitting my head on a large screw under the bleachers. Blood started pouring, and it disrupted the night of fun and games for everyone. They had to take me to the emergency room where the nurse proceeded to shave a circle on the crown of my head and give me seven stiches. That was fun! I spent weeks with an absolutely lovely bandage on the top of my head and many more months trying to grow hair back in that spot and adjusting my hairstyle to cover my baldness in the meantime. The PRICE I paid to get Bill Jones to notice me, and even THAT didn't work! I still have a thin spot in that area of my scalp; Bill always said it was to remind me that I shouldn't have been in the gym flirting with other guys! I told him that I wouldn't have been if HE had been there in the first place! Geez Louise!

Karen & Paula at EC

When I went home for Christmas break, I told my mama and Aunt Ellen that I was beginning to really like this guy named Bill Jones. I made sure they knew he was NOT a ministerial student, and I also told them that it probably wouldn't work out because he didn't seem interested in me.

Letter from Karen to Bill: July 11, 1973

I was thinking last night about how God really did put love in our hearts for each other. I remember when I first met you at school — you had no attraction to me at all (nothing personal, of course Ha!) Around December — I got to know you better and during Christmas vacation, I told Ellen one day that I liked you and wanted to date you. But I also told her that you really weren't my type, and it could never amount to anything. But by (early) January, I was falling in love with you so fast it worried me. I even prayed that I wouldn't fall for you! I also know that you weren't too crazy about me (or I wouldn't have had to chase you so much!)

I do believe that you love me, so God gave us our love. And what a love it is! I've never known such love before! You are a very large part of me, and I love you so much!"

Girls in college dormitories TALK. That's just a fact. As my heart began to lean more towards Bill, I naturally mentioned it to my friends. They began to work behind the scenes to "help" me get his attention. Unfortunately, it backfired one day and nearly crushed my spirit.

Bill was nice to me, and we would chat at times, but it was always in groups. He never sought me out when I was alone. When we returned from Christmas break, I was in the cafeteria sitting with two of my girlfriends. My back was to the window, but they saw Bill walking across the campus quad heading for the cafeteria. They told me to move to an empty table a couple of rows away from them. They could see Bill as he approached the tables with his lunch tray, but my back was to him. They kept giving me little signals as he got closer, and they were trying not to get the giggles. They were convinced that he would sit with me, and that was my hope for sure!

Bill walked right past me and sat down with them. My friends looked at me with such sadness in their eyes; they were embarrassed for me. My heart broke in my chest. It was humiliating to feel so exposed. He saw me; he knew I was there, but he chose them instead. I got up with my lunch tray and hurried to put it in the return window as I choked back the tears. My eyes were tearing up so fast, I was afraid I would trip and fall. I couldn't get out of the cafeteria fast enough. Once I was outside,

I let the tears flow, and I ran into my dormitory and down to my room.

Our dorm had a prayer room on the basement level. My broken heart needed mending, so I knew I needed to have some alone time with God. I went down to the prayer room that night and cried out to God and begged Him to take away the feelings I had for Bill. I explained to God that Bill was obviously not interested in me. Isn't it strange that we often feel the need to EXPLAIN things to a God who KNOWS EVERYTHING? I had become an embarrassment, a joke. I had made my feelings known to my friends, and now they knew that Bill did not feel the same way. To the eighteen-year-old me, it felt like the end of the world. I could not get the expressions on my friends' faces out of my mind — the "Poor Karen" look. I told God that I did NOT want to love Bill Jones; I pleaded with Him to take the longing out of my heart before my heart was completely broken. I prayed for hours, but God did not answer my prayer; the feelings remained, and my heart ached more every single day.

My miracle was coming, and it was only days away. It was coming with a "catch" though. God tricked me. Yes, you read that right. God tricked me, and I am so thankful He did!

Chapter Four

God's Trick

Emmanuel had a tradition of a winter quarter revival which began just a few days upon our return from Christmas break. Students were required to attend the Franklin Springs P.H. Church which was located on campus. Things are different now because the college has grown, and the church can no longer hold the student body. The church has a traditional "cross" shape with small wings on either side of the pulpit/choir area and a long sanctuary with pews with an aisle down the middle. When school was in session, the sanctuary was filled to the max with college students, faculty and staff, and local congregants. The rich teaching and preaching that I heard during those college years has had an immeasurable impact on me!

On the night of January 6, 1973, I am not sure where I sat during the preaching service. I was still pretty raw inside from my night of prayer a couple of days earlier. My heart was hurting, and I saw no reason to expect relief from my pain. I hoped that God would answer my prayer and remove my feelings for Bill; maybe He would do it during this revival. My friends and I usually sat near the front on the right side in the main sanctuary. We rarely sat in the wings. I do remember sitting in the right wing during the altar service, though. I will never forget THAT.

The preaching was powerful that night, and students flooded the altar to pray. The altar service ran long, and at some point, I moved to the right wing. I imagine it was because a certain young man was earnestly seeking God at the altar, and he could be clearly seen from my vantage point in the right wing. I'd like to say that I stayed late in that wing to seek God myself, but I can't lie. I was just there to watch Bill Jones. I could not take my eyes off him. He was so totally focused on God with tears streaming down his face as he looked up to Heaven. I saw Bill receive the Baptism of the Holy Spirit that night. My heart filled with joy as I saw him being beautifully blessed.

I know that many of you are not from Pentecostal backgrounds, and may have misconceptions. I won't go into too much detail at this point, but I can assure you that the experience is real. It is not just emotions run amuck. It is not simply an expression from backwoods people who cannot contain their religious ecstasy, and it is also NOT an indication of spiritual immaturity. It is a powerful, life-changing, encounter with Almighty God. It happens to people of all ages, races, educational backgrounds, and financial status. There are people from many denominations and church backgrounds who have experienced God this way with the evidence of speaking in tongues. It is a legitimate religious experience, and it is nothing to fear. I have always hoped that when people got to know me, they would understand all of this a little better. I will add that I have never been comfortable being too emotional myself. I wanted to receive the Baptism of the Holy Spirit, but I did not want to feel "out of control." In 1973, God filled me while I was simply sitting in a pew. It was a relatively quiet but life-changing experience for me, and I never felt out of control.

Human beings respond differently to all of the experiences of life. The same is true of religious experiences. Some people bawl their eyes out when they accept Christ as their personal Savior. Others seem much more reserved. One experience is not more legitimate than the other. Only God knows the hearts of those who seek Him. God needs our surrender; He does not seek to embarrass us. Sometimes God may ask us to surrender our pride in order to fill us with His anointing. Again, that is a very personal thing between God and His child. Bill didn't jump the altar or run the aisles that night. He simply sought God's power and anointing in His life, and God responded. It was a beautiful thing to behold.

As time passed, most of the congregation began to slip out quietly and go home. I was about to leave myself when I saw Bill slowly get up from the altar. My heart started pounding when he began to walk in my direction! There were probably about a dozen other students still in the wing with me, but most were behind me. I was sitting alone on one of the small pews. I fully expected him to walk past me — as he had done in the cafeteria, but he sat down beside me. He SAT DOWN BESIDE ME!

He said, ***"God did something special in my life tonight."***

I responded, ***"Yes, I know. You received the Baptism."***

Bill quietly said, ***"Yes, I did, but that's not all. I accepted a call to PREACH."***

The world stopped spinning, and my heartbeat began to slow down.

WHAT??? REALLY???

Oh no! Not that! God KNEW I didn't want to marry a preacher. He led me to give my heart away to a marine biologist or a horticulturist! I truly didn't really know what either of those professions actually entailed, but it sounded like MONEY to me, and I was okay with that! Not THIS!

I took a breath and attempted to respond appropriately.

"Oh, that's wonderful!"

I said the right words, but I can assure you that my heart was NOT in the right place. I felt that God had pulled the rug out from under my feet. Bill kept talking, but I truly cannot remember anything he said until he uttered this phrase.

"Are you hungry? Wanna go to the canteen and get a bite to eat?"

"Sure! That sounds nice."

Karen at EC

Bill Jones walked me to the small college canteen. I don't remember what we ate. All that mattered was that we were eating ***together*** — just the two of us. He was talking to ME — alone — just me. He was looking at ME — ***only me***. Right now, tears are flooding my eyes as I remember this moment. I knew it was special; I knew the world had shifted. At the time, Bill did not fully understand the significance of this moment, but I did.

God knew that I had to give my heart to Bill first. I needed to be committed BEFORE Bill accepted that call to preach. It would have been too easy for me to walk away if Bill had been one of those overly eager ministerial students looking for a piano-playing, singing candidate for a preacher's wife position!

God is SMART, and He did trick me just a little. I have forgiven Him for it, though.

From that cold night in January, we never looked back. We never looked at anyone else. Each step we took brought us closer together. By Valentine's Day we were a couple, an "item." We had fallen in love like a house on fire! Just watching him walk toward me would take my breath away.

I wrote Bill a long letter on February 21, 1973. We saw each other every day, but I wanted to bare my soul to him, and we just didn't have that many opportunities to talk alone on campus. I also didn't think I could say some of these things to his face.

By the way, when I met Bill, he was called "Billy" by his family in North Carolina. Some of his nieces and nephews call him "Uncle Billy" to this day. So, I started calling him Billy myself. During those college years, he began to refer to himself as "Bill Jones" which sounded more mature to him. He was "my Billy" for about half of our married life. When he began a season of conference leadership, I made the change and began to call him "Bill." He was fine with me calling him Billy, but I knew he preferred being called Bill by others. It was difficult for me to change, but I did.

February 21, 1973 Room 13
Jackson Hall 11:45 pm

> ***My Dearest Billy,***
>
> ***I don't guess I've written you a real letter before, but I feel that the time is right. I want you to keep this letter for future reference. Whenever you feel in doubt — read it and pray for a while. I'm sure that it will help remove the doubt.***

My emotions are all keyed up, but I'll try to keep cool and write legibly; this is one letter that I must write carefully. I feel that my whole life may depend on it.

The key to this letter is to say, William Noyel Jones, I love you. But it's not just a regular love. Billy, I love you more than I've ever loved anyone before in my life! That's no exaggeration either. I'm yours Billy — forever. All I ask is that you love me. I know that I'm no catch — but I will promise you that I'll give you all the love, warmth, and companionship that you'll ever need. I'll be a sounding board for your moody days, a shoulder to cry on when things look down. Billy, I want to go where you go — live where you live — work where you work — and be what (or part of what) you are. I want to be part of your life. I thank God every day for leading me to you. I feel unworthy of your love, but I praise God for letting me bathe in your love for a period anyway.

I don't want this to end. I love you so much; I constantly fear my heart will burst because I care so deeply! Never before have I felt such complete devotion. I love you enough to wait four years. I want to spend the rest of my life with you, Billy. I want to be not JUST a preacher's wife — but Billy Jones' wife — whether you are a minister or a ditchdigger!

I'm crying. Lord, help me. I'm crying! My mind and heart are so confused and conflicted. My God — I love you, Billy. Please — please — don't hurt me. My mind says, "Don't let him know you care so much." My heart says, "Tell him you love everything about him." I feel unsure, Billy. I trust you completely, and I have faith in you, but the devil makes me doubt sometimes.

The last thing I have to say is this: God is first in my life because I must lean on Him for strength. Your love for me is human — it may end. If it does, I have to depend on God's everlasting love to keep me going. I know that God must always remain first in your life because you're chosen to be His disciple. I never want to hurt you, Billy. I'm striving ever to be a help and not a hindrance. Please tell me if I say or do anything displeasing to you. I want to make you happy and please you.

We must pray together and separate for our relationship to last. If we both pray earnestly and strive to show ourselves approved unto God — nothing, absolutely NOTHING will keep us apart.

I never want to be first — just to share a portion of your love and your life. Give me that, and I'll be forever grateful. May God richly bless you throughout your life, and may I be a small part of that life. You're the only boy I can truthfully say that I love more than life itself. Billy, never doubt my love or my faithfulness. I'm yours and yours alone — for as long as you want me. I love you.

Forever,
Karen

We had declared our love for each other before Valentine's Day, but it had been so difficult for me to gain Bill's affection that I was unsure of myself which is evident in my letter to him. My self-confidence took a pretty big hit, and I have continued to struggle with that for most of my life. I know why God did what He did, but being rejected by Bill early on truly took the wind out of my sails.

Once we had officially declared our love and become a couple, we enjoyed walking together to the post office in Franklin Springs to check for mail. One day as we were walking back to campus, Bill said something interesting.

"Isn't it strange how God placed us together?"

"Yep! It sure is," I replied.

"I don't want to hurt your feelings or anything, but I had never really noticed you before that night. I mean, I knew who you were, but I hadn't really NOTICED you."

Well, wasn't that just a delightful thing for me to hear? Of course, I knew that he hadn't noticed me before! It had broken my heart! He went on to clarify his intent.

"God had clearly told me that I must testify and confess that I'd accepted a call to preach. I felt such an urgency to do that. When I opened my eyes and saw that you were the ONLY one in the wing, I decided to tell you. After we talked for a few minutes, it was like I really SAW you for the first time."

I was blown away by that statement because that was NOT reality.

> ***"Billy, there were probably ten or twelve other students sitting in that wing with me that night! I wasn't the only person there!***
>
> ***"No!"*** he insisted. ***"You were the ONLY one. That's why I went to YOU!"***

Neither one of us said anything else as God settled the truth of that encounter with us. God made sure that Bill did not SEE anyone but ME. He wanted Bill to notice ME because I was part of the plan. After that conversation, we ***never*** doubted that God brought us together miraculously. We ***never*** doubted what God had done that night in the Franklin Springs Church.

Bill spent the rest of his life encouraging me and trying to strengthen my confidence. Many of my friends have a hard time believing this, but Bill understood it completely. The heartbreak I felt at my inability to attract Bill, along with other disappointments, caused me to pull in and become more of an introvert. If I have accomplished anything in my adult life, it is because Bill encouraged me and pushed me out of my shell. I couldn't even write this book without sensing his devotion to me.

My vanity would have liked for Bill to have "noticed" me and pursued me in the traditional sense. Knowing that God had orchestrated our relationship and had planted love in our hearts for each other kept us together through some of the heartbreaking trials we would face on our journey. God's way of joining us may not have been our choice, but it certainly provided the strong foundation we would later need.

One of the best compliments Bill ever gave me (many years after we were married) was when he said that I had never given him a reason to be ashamed of me. He said I always made him proud. Pleasing him was the one thing I wanted the most.

> **Letter from Bill: August 27, 1973**
>
> ***I'm so proud of you, Karen — you are the most beautiful and loving woman in the world. You do make me so very happy… I'm very proud of you and your love for me, and I always want to be worthy of that love. I'm going to do everything in my ability to make you happy and keep you happily in love with me. You are the***

> ***most important thing in my life. Only my duty to serve God will come before you.***
>
> ***I feel that we were made just for each other. I do thank God for you. I think — no, I know that God has a work for us to do together. I think you are an excellent type to be a minister — THIS minister's wife. Just pray for me and us. I love you with all my heart, and I know you love me, too. That makes me one happy man.***

Yes, God tricked us. We were on different paths, but after January 6, 1973, there was only ***ONE*** path — ***OURS***. We never looked back; we only looked ahead. Our journey together was just beginning, and no matter where it led, we would be taking it together, and that is all that mattered.

Chapter Five

Growing in Love

Letter from Karen: February 27, 1973

I'm yours, and if it's ten years before you're ready — I'll wait. Please remember that. Sure, you may be a "poor preacher," but if God thinks enough of you to personally choose you for His service — then I feel downright honored to have you say, "Karen, I do love you." Never, ever think that you're not good enough or rich enough for me. I've always been poor, and the love you give to me is the richest thing I'll ever have. I feel honored and thankful to share your love — whether it lasts for a year — or a lifetime. Whatever you decide — I'll be willing to make it work. I'm yours — forever Billy. I love you.

Letter from Bill: July 2, 1973

Karen, I love you with every inch of my heart, and I know that God has brought us together and made my love this strong. So don't worry — whether I make you my wife next summer, or if we have to wait two years — you are the one and only woman I love, and the only one I ever will love. I mean it.

Bill and Karen
EC banquet

Once the love bug bit; we were both goners! From mid-January to early June of 1973, we spent every possible minute together while trying to keep our grades up and stay involved in campus activities. It was a whirlwind to be sure! I was making certain that everyone in my family knew about my new beau! In describing Bill to one of my uncles, I mentioned that Bill had a rather large head. He asked me a question that I couldn't really answer.

"How big is it? What size hat does he wear?"

Bill had told me that they had to special order a football helmet for him. It was bigger than anything the school had ever needed before. I didn't know anything about hat sizes, so when my uncle asked me, this was my response.

"I don't know, maybe a size ten?"

Well, once I told Bill that I had given his hat size as "ten," he had a fit.

"What in the world? Your uncle must think I'm some sort of monster!"

He explained to me that he wore a 7 7/8 hat or an XXL. I never made that mistake again, but we laughed for over fifty years about Bill's "size ten" head!

As June approached, the reality of being apart for the summer weighed heavily on us. Bill would go back to North Carolina with his folks, and I would head back to Virginia with mine. Approximately 350 miles would separate us, and about 5-6 hours of driving time. Kids today simply cannot relate. We had no cell phones, and long distance was expensive! Our parents were still struggling to pay their regular bills. Not seeing each other for weeks at a time seemed impossible. We had become accustomed to seeing each other EVERY SINGLE DAY. We still had an occasional class together; we ate meals together when we could; we went to church together, studied together, and -occasionally- went on double dates with friends.

Bill and I both worked in the college work-study program. After my initial stint in the admissions office, I worked as a secretary for college faculty members. I had been a fast and accurate typist in high school, and that helped me to be a valuable asset to faculty members who needed quite a bit of typing done. Bill worked on the maintenance crew and sometimes rode on the town's garbage truck. He LOVED that particular job! LOL! Working and going to college at the same time kept us busy, but we were never too busy for each other. We had no car and no money, so our dating experiences were few and far between. We could simply "be" together for free, and we did as much of that as possible. Just the idea of a three-month separation was killing us; it was nearly unbearable.

Over the summer, he drove a gas truck around Clinton and surrounding towns, and I worked at The Natural Bridge of Virginia. I got my first job there at the ripe age of fifteen and worked there until Bill and I were married. The pay was pretty lousy, but it was close to my house, and I got to work with several of my high school classmates. I started out as a bus girl in the cafeteria and was promoted to the cashier position which paid more. During that LONG summer of 1973, I worked as a soda jerk in the soda fountain. When Bill would come to visit, he would see me scooping ice cream, making real milkshakes, malts, and floats. It sounds like fun, but it was a NASTY job! I had sticky ice cream all over me by the end of the shift. To this day, I do NOT like chocolate ice cream. Nothing, and I mean NOTHING is as rock hard as a new bucket of chocolate ice cream. It is like trying to scoop CEMENT! We would always run low when a bus full of school children would come in, and they all yelled for CHOCOLATE! What a nightmare!

Summer 1973 Goodbyes

As the spring quarter ended, Bill and I prepared to say our goodbyes. We promised each other that we would write letters frequently. We kept that promise, and I have two boxes of love letters to prove it! They were a lifeline to us. We wrote each other every single day, sometimes two or three times a day. His letters smelled like gasoline because he often wrote them during times when he was dumping gas at a station. I wrote on whatever stationary I had, and even wrote a couple on napkins from Natural Bridge! I learned how to fold the bags from the gift shop into makeshift envelopes which worked really well! You can't accuse me of not being creative!

We didn't care about the smell or the stationary. We only cared about the words we were reading. Our souls thirsted for those words; they were like crisp, clean water in the middle of the desert! Separation was killing us; we were meant to be together, and we knew it with every inch of our being.

> **Note from Bill on the day we left Emmanuel for the summer of 1973**
>
> ***I love you with all my heart, and I'll miss you so much — I miss you already. However, I know God brought us together, and if we stay true to Him, we'll make it.***
>
> **Letter from Bill: June 27, 1973**
>
> ***I didn't get a letter from you today so my lunch hour was miserable. I miss you so much, baby, and my job is tiring. So, all I do is think about you while I'm driving,***
>
> **Letter from Bill: July 16, 1973**
>
> ***I got three letters from you today. The one with the "Love Is" drawings was cute. Maybe if you don't make it as an English major, you could be an artist!***
>
> **Letter from Bill: August 1, 1973**
>
> ***Hello Darling,***
>
> ***I'm in Garland, NC again, and boy is it hot here! It must be 95 in the shade. There are thunder clouds building everywhere. I got three letters from you. The first two were great, but the last one kinda made me feel bad. I'm sorry that you got so upset and cried cause you thought that I couldn't come (to visit.)***

Sometimes the postal service just couldn't handle the load! We would miss a day without letters and then get three in one day! My daddy loved teasing me about it.

"Why do you want to check the mailbox? You think "that ole boy" is going to write you again?"

Bill and I always laughed about how Daddy called him "that ole boy" for YEARS! It seemed that way to us, but I know that he called him Bill after we were married. He accepted Bill as another son and loved him dearly. Daddy was quite concerned about us falling in love and being so serious at our young age. He knew what we would face. He and Mama married at the tender age of seventeen, and I was born when they were eighteen. They also had financial struggles, but their marriage survived for seventy years — until Mama went to Heaven.

A day without a letter was like a day without sunshine. Bill's mama told him he was too "mopey" and grumpy. Daddy said the same about me. He said Bill and I spent too much time together at school; he said it would be like marrying my brother! Uhhh…NOPE, it was ***NOTHING*** like THAT! It was wonderful, and we could hardly wait to be man and wife. Unfortunately, there were obstacles in our way, and challenges loomed ahead that we could not even imagine.

Chapter Six

The Summer of '73 — Part I

Letter from Karen: June 3, 1973

I started crying in the car after I read your letter. Barry (my brother) said that you told him that was why you made me wait to open it because you knew I'd cry. You know me pretty well, don't you, Jones? I held it back because I didn't want to cry in front of your parents or you. You're probably beginning to think that I'm a crybaby — but nothing means anything more than you, and the thought of us being 350 miles apart makes me cry. But it's like you've told me before — God has put us together and as long as we trust Him — nothing will keep us apart.

I feel like somebody has ripped my heart out and left it in North Carolina. Part of me is missing. The first sentence I said when Mama woke me up in our driveway was, "I wish I was back in Georgia."

Letter from Bill: June 4, 1973

Last night in the motel, Mom and I talked about us. I told her I really missed you. She said that you talked like you'd miss me too! She knows we're really in love.

I really do miss you, Baby. It really didn't hit me until last night that you were gone, and I wouldn't see you for three weeks. I just sat in the room and looked at the pictures Dad made of us. I wanted to grab you, hold you, and kiss you, but your father was ready to go; everybody was hot, and if you had started crying, I probably would have too.

Thus began the summer of 1973. We had to readjust to living at home with our parents. Unpacking from college, getting settled into our old bedrooms, and returning to our regular jobs consumed most of our time. We tried to call each other weekly; we took turns to keep costs down. Our family phone hung on the wall in the kitchen; Bill's family phone was on a table in the family room, just outside the bathroom. He could pick up their phone and go into the bathroom for a bit of privacy. I couldn't take our phone ANYWHERE, and there was NO privacy! We knew that our parents could overhear our conversations. Even if they said they weren't listening, we knew they were! It's what parents do. Our letters were filled with "love" talk because our phone conversations had to be rather "business like" and "sterile." We managed because we simply loved hearing each other's voice.

Letter from Karen: June 20, 1973

After this year of school, we'll have a lot of decisions to make and then go our separate ways again — possibly for as long as two years. That's a horrible thought. We've been separated for three weeks now, and I've hated it! I can't be truly happy unless you're with me, but that's because I love you with all of my heart and soul. I want to spend the rest of my life loving you too.

By the end of June, we knew that we could not continue to be apart if we could help it. Bill began to talk about marriage plans, and I was in agreement with him.

Letter from Bill: June 30, 1973

You said that you had been praying about us a lot — so have I! I would like for us to get married in the summer following next year. I know that's saying a lot, and I haven't even mentioned it to Mom yet. Of course, a lot of planning and praying will have to transpire between now and then. As always with married people,

our problem will be money. Also, we would have to figure out how you could get your BA degree.

Before we even mention it to our parents, I want us to discuss it fully and really look at it closely. All I know is that I love you and I want you to be my wife "as soon as possible." I just don't feel right when I'm away from you. If it weren't for the Lord helping me (and sometimes it seems as though I won't let Him do that) I wouldn't make it.

What we do must be in God's perfect will for me and you. I do feel that He brought us together, and "what God hath joined together, let no man put asunder." AMEN!

Letter from Bill: July 28, 1973

I've been doing a lot of thinking and praying about us. I don't want to be away from you anymore than I have to. If there is any way possible, I would like for us to get married after next year at Emmanuel. I know we would probably run into a lot of troubles, but I don't think I could stand two years like this. I want to pray about it, and think about it — OK?

Letter from Karen: August 7, 1973

Billy, let's get married as soon as we possibly can! If that's June — fine! I love you, and I can hardly bear living without you anymore. There will be hard times, but I'm willing to bear them all with you. I love you so much.

Letter from Karen: August 25, 1973

It's started raining outside, and everyone is asleep except me. There are times like these when I long for us to be married. To be able to reach out in the night and find you there close by. The warmth of your arms on cold or stormy nights. There's so much more to marriage than sex — the closeness of each other, getting to know the little things about each other.

Our letters became more focused on future plans. If ever there was a BUDGET planner, it was Bill Jones. In later years, some of our church members started calling him the "Budget King." It described him perfectly. In our early years of marriage, I often chafed under his strict budgeting. I worked hard and brought a significant income into the family. I thought I needed a bit more freedom in my spending. Bill firmly believed that all of the money was "ours" and should go into our joint account. He managed the checkbook, and I just never had any money unless I asked him for it. That didn't suit me very well, and we had WORDS about money quite often.

The solution was for me to have side hustles that gave me spending money for which I didn't have to account. I would cut hair, give perms, bake and sell cookies to a local restaurant, and sell Avon for years! I started selling items online in 2020, and I still do that. My daddy always had more than one job, so I suppose I take after him in that. Each couple has to find its way regarding finances. What worked for us won't work for everyone, but Bill always handled our finances with integrity. I trusted him completely, and he never failed me. He was TIGHT with a nickel, but he made sure that our needs were met. We didn't always have what we wanted, but we had what we needed.

I saw his planning and budgeting skills at work for the first time during that summer of '73. He sent me multiple letters filled with columns of income vs. expenditures. He wrote multiple letters to the business manager of the college asking questions about available jobs for us. Thankfully, the college was small, and the business manager sincerely cared for us and wanted to help us out. God was in our corner for sure!

Two issues were of great concern. Bill was planning to stay in Georgia and be a part of the very first four-year degree program at Emmanuel. The college was starting a new School of Christian Ministries. The plan was for us to graduate with our AA degrees in June of 1974, get married, and return to Franklin Springs to live. Bill would complete his junior and senior years in the School of Christian Ministries and earn his undergraduate degree in 1976. One major concern was that he would not have as many student loans available to him since it was a new program of study for the college.

The second HUGE issue was my education. We both desperately wanted me to be able to finish college and earn my BA in English Education. We knew that a teaching career would help us financially. Bill often told people that I had always supported his "preaching habit." That line usually got a good laugh, but there was much truth in it. I taught school for forty years, and God certainly used my career to help us through many lean financial stretches. We had hoped that I would be able to go to the University of Georgia since it was only thirty miles away from Franklin Springs. The problem is that we found out my time at Emmanuel would not count toward residency requirements for in-state tuition. There was no way we could afford out-of-state tuition.

If we could not marry in June of 1974, I would have to stay in Virginia to complete my degree while Bill finished his in Georgia. By the end of that 1973 summer, we both knew that we could not wait that long.

> ***But if they cannot control themselves, they should marry, for it is better to marry than to burn with passion.*** **(1 Corinthians 7:9 NIV)**

To be perfectly honest, we were BURNING with passion! We loved each other desperately. I believe our parents understood this. They all expressed their concerns, but they saw the course of action that needed to be taken. Asking us to wait for two more years would be inviting disaster. They were wiser than we, and they knew that we would not be able to refrain for much longer.

Summer 1973 Visit

When I hear people say they dated for six years, eight years, or ten years before they married, I often wonder how they did it. Did they feel the same passion we felt? In today's culture, most people don't expect to wait until marriage to consummate the relationship. I will be very transparent here and say that we were struggling constantly with desire. I won't lie; we went further than we should have, but maturity has taught me that we were not alone in this. We were both virgins when we married, and we stayed faithful to each other for our entire marriage. I am thankful for that, and I am glad that our parents gave us their blessing to marry in June of 1974.

Letter from Bill: August 16, 1973

In exactly two weeks and one day, I'll be quitting work. In two weeks and six days, I'll be coming to get you. In ten months, I hope to make you my wife, and I'm gonna do just that too! I love you!

Letter from Bill: August 17, 1973

I love you so very, very much. You truly are the woman of my dreams. I praise God for you and your love. I promise you again that I will do my best to always merit that love. I must close. Just remember that I love you with all my heart, Mrs. Jones. Yours forever and ever, Billy.

We were getting more and more excited as we realized our dream of getting married in 1974 was becoming a real possibility. Our parents were on board, and Bill was busier than ever trying to figure out the finances. We were so desperate to get married that we would have lived on beans and water if necessary, and it just about came to that at times! Nothing mattered as much as being together; we knew we could overcome any obstacle as long as we did it ***together***.

By the end of the summer of 1973, we realized that something far more troubling than the lack of finances might stand in our way. It would become the "thing" that cast a shadow over most of our married lives.

Letter from Karen: August 26, 1973

Take care of yourself and remember that we're getting married in June- regardless! You'd just better tell your old kidneys that Karen isn't going to put up with any nonsense from them. They won't spoil our plans!!

Chapter Seven

Summer of '73 — Part II

Letter from Bill: June 25, 1973

I felt like crying on the way back (from Virginia). I felt so good when I was with you, but now my back is killing me. I'm so afraid my kidneys are acting up again. I haven't felt this bad for over a year. If I don't feel better by later this week, I'm going to go to the doctor. I was up last night from about 1:00 — 1:30 in the bathroom. I went to bed at 11:00 because I was so tired after driving all the way back. Pray for me, OK? I don't want to have to go back to the doctor and start taking pills and shots.

Letter from Bill: June 26, 1973

I feel much better today. I still don't feel quite right though. I guess all the work last week plus all of the riding just tired me out more than I thought. If it doesn't clear up soon; however, I'm still gonna go see the doctor. I remember what you said your mother told you about not getting involved with a sickling, so I'm gonna see if I can't stay well cause I don't want to lose you. I love you so much that I think it would kill me if I lost you. Anyway, what I wanted to tell you was, don't worry about me. Just pray for me, and I know that God can work things out.

Letter from Bill: August 17, 1973

I'm going to go see the doctor next week. I'm sorta worried. I shouldn't have waited this long to go see him, but I'm afraid I'm a terrible procrastinator when it comes to going to doctors. Baby, I just got to be well of this kidney thing. We can't afford doctor's bills for me. Pray for me real earnestly, OK?

Letter from Bill: August 23, 1973

Honey, I never dreamed of anything like this. I'm in a daze. I hate that it is working out like this for me. I love you, and I need you, but I hate to worry you with this. But I am being honest and telling you all that I know. I may be having some trouble for the rest of my life with my kidneys. I didn't know this when I asked you to marry me; if I had, I would've told you. Honey, I love you with all my heart, and I want very much for you to be my wife. This was a hardship that I had not planned on. What I'm trying to say is that I still love you with all my heart, but I want you to be happy with me and still want to be my wife.

God has called me to preach, and I'll never doubt that even if my kidneys fall out. I also feel that God has brought us together and made our love as strong as it is. I still want us to get married next June. I don't know what will work out about my kidneys, but I do know that God can do all things. We will just have to plan on and trust God to work things out.

Letter from Karen: August 26, 1973

I love you so much, Honey. There's nowhere in the world I'd rather be right now than in Clinton with you in my arms. I want to put my arms around you — hold you close and tell you that everything is going to be alright. I know that God is going to work things out for us. He has too much in store for you to let you get sick — right?"

After we had become a couple, Bill shared with me that he had developed a persistent kidney infection in high school. He played football, and it hindered his ability to play at times. He didn't think it was anything serious, and he didn't expect to have any more trouble, so we never thought about it further.

Over the course of the summer of 1973, he began to have more symptoms, and they would not go away. The more concerned he became, the more worrying I did. My mama wasn't being unkind (June 26 letter), but she knew how difficult things could be if Bill did have chronic health issues. She didn't know how serious we had become about getting married, so she tried to advise me to take it easy until I knew more. Any caring mother would have done the same.

In all honesty, I had no idea what was ahead of us. If I had been able to look down the road in a crystal ball and see everything that was coming, would I have run the other way? I wish I could stand tall and say, "Absolutely not!" I won't be dishonest with you; I don't know what I would have done. The road ahead would be heartbreaking in many places; I'm not sure I would have chosen to fight the good fight and move ahead at the age of eighteen. I'm not sure I had enough courage or fortitude at that point.

Jezebel

At the end of the summer, Bill drove to Virginia to load up his "new" and freshly painted (dark green) Rambler station wagon with my college luggage. The car had been sitting in his daddy's yard for a long time and needed quite a bit of work! Over the summer, his Uncle Jesse had put a new motor in it. Bill and his daddy fixed a radiator leak, put new tires on the car, had the seats covered, and had a friend put on a fresh coat of paint. Bill named her "Jezebel" because she was a "painted lady." Bill had nicknames for EVERYBODY and EVERYTHING! It was one of the things I adored about him over the years. Jezebel may not have been fancy, but she served us well for the first few years of our marriage. We were just so happy that we finally had WHEELS!

The plan was for me to spend the last week of summer vacation with his family in North Carolina. There were still family members to meet, and since we were officially engaged (ring and all) at that point, it would give me some time to get to know his parents better. We were thrilled at the prospect of spending that week together before the hustle and bustle of school started!

Letter from Bill: August 29, 1973

Hello Baby,

I love you, and I need you here with me now so that I can talk to you and snuggle you up and get strength from you. I went to the nurse again today, and my condition is about the same, so I talked to her about getting a specialist immediately instead of waiting until Christmas. After all, it would not be fair to you, us, or me to wait. We need to know just what this kidney infection is and what problems I will have in the future with it. Cause you could not plan a wedding or future jobs confidently without knowing what my kidney trouble is exactly.

There is one specialist in town, and the nurse is to call and make an appointment for me with him today. I also decided to quit work this afternoon. I'll lose one week's pay, but if I can get an appointment with the specialist and get squared up, it will be worth losing pay, right?

Please, please pray for me cause Satan has really been trying to get me down with this. I got home from work yesterday and cried like a dummy. But everything seemed to look so bleak. All I could think about was that if I was sick for a long time, or had large doctor's bills, or couldn't go to get you, or a million other dismal thoughts.

But two things kept me going:

1. *The knowledge of God's love*
2. *The knowledge of your love for me.*

Please Honey, don't stop loving me. I want and need your love so much right now.

I'm hoping and praying that nothing will interfere with our plans for going back to school together. I hope that if I have to be hospitalized that they can finish the necessary tests in a week's time (next week).

I have an appointment to see him (kidney specialist) again September 10th (Monday after we get back from your house). By then he will have the results of the blood tests, x-rays, and cultures, so

> ***he might be able to diagnose the problem's source. He has given me some pills and said that I would probably be on medication for some time.***

If we'd had even an inkling of how *MUCH* medication Bill would have to take and for how *LONG*, we would never have believed it.[1]

1 see Appendix A

Chapter Eight

Sophomore Year

I was incredibly excited and nervous about that week with Bill and his family. I wanted to measure up to everyone's expectations of me. On Monday of that week, Bill and I got ready for the follow-up appointment with the specialist. I got comfortable in the waiting room as Bill went back to see the doctor. We both thought he would probably prescribe a new medication or treatment, and then we could get on with a day of fun together. After a few moments, the nurse came out and told me that the doctor would like to speak to me as well. I had seen enough medical dramas on television and movies to know that her announcement did NOT bode well for us. Bill and I were only engaged, and the doctor wanted to see ***ME*** as well.

We sat side-by-side across from the doctor, and he began his explanation.

> ***"Bill, we took x-rays of your kidneys so that we could better see what is going on. We have the results. The problem is that the x-rays don't show ANY kidneys!"***

Bill and I looked at each other; we didn't know what to make of that statement.

The doctor then chuckled a bit nervously, as he continued.

> ***"Well, you're sitting here, and you are breathing, so you must have at least ONE kidney somewhere, but we need to find it. We want***

> ***to admit you to the hospital TODAY. We need to do a scope and get inside for a better look to find your kidney."***

Our world began to crumble just a bit. This was more serious than we had ever dreamed. I was also on the edge of panic because Bill was going into the hospital, and I would be ALONE with his mama and daddy! I didn't know if he would be in the hospital for a day or for the week! It was NOT a good situation. Bill was distraught. He wanted to spend the week with me, NOT in a hospital bed being poked and prodded. He was also scared. Remember, we were both only eighteen years old, and this was a frightening situation. What ELSE might they find as they searched around his body? My heart aches when I think about us — so young — facing such dire news in that doctor's office.

Bill ended up spending most of the week in the hospital. I do remember one humorous moment when they brought Bill back after the procedure. He was groggy from the anesthesia, and his sweet mama was in the hospital room with me. Bill began to twist and turn as the drugs wore off and the pain kicked in. The sheet began to fall off the bed, and he was exposed quite a bit! I'm sure Pinkie hadn't moved THAT FAST in many years! She grabbed that sheet and SECURED it over him lickity split! Neither of us said anything, but that memory tickles me to this day.

After the doctor had run more tests and done the scope, he met with the two of us again. Bill had been born with only one kidney. It was misplaced, and they could not get a good look at it with the technology available in 1973. He said there were other birth anomalies as well, but he didn't think they would be problematic. He explained to us that Bill might spend his entire life without any problems from that kidney. He also said that some people have THREE kidneys, and they usually have more issues! If Bill had not had the kidney infections, they might never have known he only had one. He tried to reassure us and encourage us to go ahead and get married. He did end the conversation with a little "by the way" comment.

> ***"Sometimes kidney problems can lead to difficulties conceiving, so if you try to get pregnant for a year without results, you might want to get it checked out."***

He gave Bill more medication and instructions and sent us on our way. We were stunned but relieved that Bill was getting out of the hospital. The doctor had been more encouraging than we expected, so we left in pretty good spirits. I think we both thought that since God had called him to preach and brought us together that everything was going to be alright. Looking back, I know we had strong faith, but we were also young and a bit naïve. God was with us, but everything wasn't going to be "alright."

He came home the day before we were scheduled to drive back to Georgia. That night in Clinton was a busy one! Family came over for a dinner — a little bit of a "meet and greet" for me. Bill's sweet mama had let me help her with a banana pudding. I am embarrassed to admit it, but I could barely boil water at that point! Bill knew, but I was embarrassed for his mother to know that I was so totally inept in the kitchen. I had taken a home economics course in high school and could do a few things by recipe, but cooking was not interesting to me, and my mama had NO patience for me in the kitchen, so I just stayed in my room and read books! Daddy had even asked me once if Bill knew I couldn't "open a can." That was an exaggeration — you may not KNOW my daddy! He loves to tease folks, and the man has LINES no one else has even written yet! Bill loved to cook, and he was a GREAT cook! He could have been a chef if he'd wanted to. He told me he wasn't marrying me to COOK! It was never an issue for us.

Pinkie told me everything to do. When the family gathered that night, she made a BIG deal about the banana pudding that "Karen made." I knew the truth, and SHE knew the truth, but she was making me shine in front of the family! Her kindness to me made me fall in love with her that night. She was a special lady indeed, and I thank God for such a precious memory of her.

After the meal was over and everyone left for home, Bill and I had to get our things together and pack the car because we needed to head back to Georgia the next morning. Pinkie interrupted us on a couple of occasions reminding Bill where the important papers were. She even told him songs that she wanted at her funeral! I will admit that it seemed rather odd at the time. Bill said, "Mama, don't be so morbid!" We just kept on packing our things.

The next morning was a bit rainy and dreary. Floyd and Pinkie were planning to take their small boat and drive to Bill's sister's house for a little fishing after we left for Georgia. I went out to the car and Bill came a couple of minutes later. He was concerned because Pinkie was standing at the sink crying. I told him to go back in and hug her one more time, and he did. When he got back in the car, he said, "That's so strange. She didn't cry when she left me in Georgia the first time!" We assumed it was because Bill and I were leaving together, and she knew that her "baby boy" was in love and would be getting married in less than a year. She came out on the little back porch in the rain and watched us drive away; it was a melancholy scene for sure. I started to say something to Bill about that, but decided against it since her crying had upset him.

We drove seven hours to get back to the college and got busy unloading the car. A student walked up and said that Mr. Henson (the men's advisor) wanted to see us in his apartment. We thought we were in trouble or something, so we walked over to the men's dorm very nervously. Shaking in our boots would be more like it! We had stopped at Hartwell Lake before we got back to school to do a little kissing. Yep, we were indeed guilty and thought we'd been discovered! Emmanuel was a Christian school, and the rules for the students were fairly strict. Things are much different now, and I know the intent was to help keep us out of trouble! We were teen-agers, and our hormones were RAGING! I am thankful for that now, but most of us resented those restrictions at the time.

When we walked in, Mr. Henson was very sweet and quiet. He smiled and welcomed us into his apartment.

> ***"Karen, please take Bill's hand."***

Physical contact was frowned upon at school, so that request took us by surprise. I reached out and took Bill's hand in mind.

> Mr. Henson softly said, ***"Bill, your parents were in a car accident today. Your father's okay; your mother isn't. You may use my phone to call home."***

Bill's hands were shaking as he made the call. Whoever answered the phone broke down and could not tell Bill what had happened. Someone else got on the line and told Bill that another college student on her way back to school in North Carolina had run a stop sign. She hit his parents'

Volkswagen van on the passenger side. The van did not have seat belts, and Pinkie was thrown through the windshield. The van flipped over on her, and she was killed instantly. The doctor said that the impact of hitting the windshield killed her. The accident happened near an elementary school, and students in the playground came and tried to ease the van off her lifeless body.

When he got the news, Bill almost collapsed. I grabbed him and held him. He broke and sobbed in my arms as Mr. Henson stood quietly by. We just stood and cried together for several minutes. I cried for the lovely lady who had shown me such grace, and I cried to see this young man so broken in my embrace. What a maelstrom of emotions we had experienced in a few days! The week we had expected to enjoy running around the county seeing relatives and old school friends had turned into a week of hospital tests and shocking revelations! The start of our sophomore year was interrupted with the devastating news of Pinkie's death. Bill's world (and mine) had taken some BIG HITS in a very short period of time, and it was difficult for us to process everything.

I didn't know Pinkie very well, and I grieved because I would never have any more time with her. That week alone with Pinkie while Bill was in the hospital was it. I was upset at the time because I couldn't be with Bill, but since then I have seen that week as a gift from God. We are often shocked along this journey we call "life," but it is comforting to look back and see God's hands at work when we thought we are walking alone. Time has a way of changing our perspective and turning many disappointments and obstacles into blessings.

One of Bill's uncles paid for both of us to fly back to North Carolina for Pinkie's funeral. Bill may have gained a fiancé at the young age of eighteen, but he also lost his beloved mother at that tender age. Bill's dad was not seriously injured in the crash; the steering wheel had prevented him from going through the windshield. We arrived back at the house to see Floyd in a state of shock. He would sit in his chair and cry with very little response to anything else going on around him. I thought his parents were old because my parents were so young. Pinkie and Floyd were about the same age as my grandparents. She was only fifty-nine years old when she died. Someone from the church called to ask the family about songs for Pinkie's funeral. Bill immediately spoke up with a couple of songs that Pinkie had just told us about the night before the wreck! It was during one of those odd interruptions of hers while we were trying to pack for our trip! A little bit later one of the older siblings asked Floyd about insurance documents they would need. Floyd just shook his head and cried; he simply could not process what was happening. Bill got up and went to the table his mother had shown him when she told him about "important documents." There were the insurance papers!

Bill and I frequently talked about the strange things that happened during that twenty-four-hour period. Pinkie had told us the songs she wanted at her funeral. She made sure that Bill knew where the important documents were. She seemed unusually upset when we left the house that next morning and even stood out in the drizzly rain to watch us drive away. We are absolutely certain that the Holy Spirit was preparing her for something. I don't believe that she knew she was going to die, but God was urging her to get her house in order; she was being prompted supernaturally. She was a faithful woman of God, and she recognized God's voice and the prompting of the Holy Spirit. I think she cried when we left because she was concerned that maybe WE would have an accident on the way back to school. She knew — spiritually— that SOMETHING was about to happen. Nothing takes God by surprise, and if we are tuned in to His direction and recognize His voice when He speaks, He will go before us and prepare us for what lies ahead.

I remember at one point Bill and I went and sat outside in the yard for a few moments of quiet. He suddenly sobbed aloud — even more racked with pain than he had been at the initial news! I held him and let him cry a bit before he could talk. He choked out that he remembered the prayer he had prayed as a boy; I mentioned it in chapter one. He was very close to his mother, and he knew she was older than his friends' moms. He had asked God to please keep her alive until he was grown and on his own.

He looked at me with tears streaming down his face.

> ***"God honored my prayer! I have asked you to be my wife, and we will be married in less than a year. I am on my own now. Who knows if God intended to take Mama earlier? I don't know! I only know that He answered my prayer and kept her with me until I had you. I don't think I could stand this loss if I were on my own."***

Flying back to school and moving on with such a serious loss was not easy, but Bill did the best he could. God strengthened him. There were many tears yet unshed; he felt the loss of his mama deeply. Pinkie's influence on Bill was evident throughout his life. I have to believe that she could see who he became and was so proud of him. I "saw" her in Bill many times over the years; her legacy was a powerful one. Bill had a tender heart, and he was never ashamed to cry. One morning not too long ago, I walked into the living room, and he was sitting in his recliner with tears in his eyes.

"I can't remember what Mama's voice sounded like."

To my knowledge we have no videos or recordings of her voice. My heart ached for him, and I hugged him and kissed his forehead. There was nothing I could say or do to alleviate his pain. It had been fifty-two years since he'd lost her. The pain of **not** remembering the sound of his mother's voice had brought tears to his eyes.

That loss was a profound one.

The fall of 1973 was a heavy one for us, but our sophomore year of college was a hurricane of activity! I was the college yearbook editor, and Bill was the business manager (a fitting job for him). I began my job as secretary to David Hopkins, the professor of the English class where Bill and I first met! I typed a great deal of his doctoral dissertation that year. David was also the faculty advisor for the yearbook, so sometimes he would let me do yearbook activities when I completed the typing for him. Many years later David went on to serve as the president of Emmanuel College (as Dr. David Hopkins) and write a wonderful history of the school. He included a couple of paragraphs about us in the book which meant a great deal to us. We thank God for the long friendship we have enjoyed over the years.

Outstanding ECSCM Alumnus

Bill served as the president of the student ministerial association. He earned many honors that year for his academic work as well as his leadership abilities. Years later he would be named ***Outstanding Alumnus of the Emmanuel College School of***

Christian Ministries which was a great honor. He was a go-getter and excelled in everything he did! I was always incredibly proud of him and his accomplishments.

EC Sophomore Year

We were both busy with other school clubs and functions. Emmanuel chose a few students each year to serve as ushers and hostesses for school events. These students were chosen for their leadership abilities and their willingness to represent the school well. I served as a hostess, and Bill was an usher. We often "worked" alumni events, school events, and community events on campus. That kept us busy as well, but we enjoyed every opportunity to just be together.

In our FREE time—not much of that—we planned our wedding. Mama started making my bridesmaids' dresses on her sewing machine in Virginia. We bought my wedding dress at a clearance sale and paid more for the veil than the dress! I chose a unique wedding invitation that would have a photo of us on the front; I'd never seen one like that before. We had the photo taken by the college yearbook photographer. I still love that photo, and it hangs in our bedroom to this day. Ladies from my church were going to make the cake. We only had cake, nuts, mints, and punch. That was all we could afford.

Wedding Invitation Photo

Truthfully, most of my relatives and friends had simpler weddings back then. We didn't do the full sit-down dinner with music and dancing. In fact, in either of our Pentecostal Holiness churches in 1974, a reception with dancing would have been scandalous! Times have certainly changed. Since my parents paid for the wedding, I am glad things were simpler then. I think our wedding was as nice as it needed to be, and it did not strain our finances too much. The MARRIAGE is FAR more important than the ceremony anyway, and I hope couples will begin to put more emphasis on that. It is not unheard of these days for marriages to fall apart before they have finished paying for the wedding! That is heartbreaking.

Spring quarter was coming to an end, and we were again facing a time apart. The GREAT news was that Bill would go to North Carolina, and I would go to Virginia but only for a week or so. He and his family would come to Virginia several days before our wedding. We could hardly wait! The clock was ticking, and we were about to become Mr. and Mrs. Bill Jones. Let the fireworks begin!

Chapter Nine

Marry Me, Bill!

I don't really remember much about my graduation from Emmanuel; our upcoming marriage consumed my thoughts and my energy! Bill and I separated without too much angst because it would only be a little over a week before I would see him again. Paula was getting married first; she beat me to the draw with scheduling the church! I was a bridesmaid in her wedding on June 8, 1974, and she came back from her honeymoon to be a bridesmaid in mine on June 15. God bless our church congregation — TWO Saturday weddings one week apart! The same pastor, the same organist, the same cake bakers, the same attendees (with different families of course). After decades as a pastor's wife, I know exactly how exhausting that must have been! They probably re-scheduled some vacations as well. Again, I say," God bless 'em!"

Paula's wedding to Billy Griffin was beautiful. It only made me more excited about my wedding to MY BILLY one week away! Our church had a long altar that went across the front which made wedding processionals slightly awkward. My precious Grandaddy Ben built a set of steps and a "bridge" that Bill and I could walk over the altar together. I was the oldest grandchild on my mama's side, and I know that Grandaddy Rice spoiled me as much as he could. He was a natural story teller, and that gift was passed on to me. He is also the one who first encouraged me to be a teacher.

"Karen, teachers make a good pension! You should be a teacher."

You have NO IDEA how grateful Bill and I were for that advice. That pension served us well for many years, and I depend on it today!

Wedding Day

After Paula and Billy drove off for their honeymoon; I jumped headfirst into one of the most exciting weeks of my life. Bill and his family arrived from North Carolina. We picked up tuxedos and checked on floral arrangements. It was difficult for Bill to be fitted properly (52" chest and 36" arms), and he was supposed to have a black jacket while the ushers had white. They mistakenly ordered white for him as well which upset him, but it was too late for them to correct it. They did not keep jackets that size in stock. The sleeves on the one they sent were too short, but we weren't going to postpone the wedding for that!

Letter from Bill: August 15, 1973

Honey, I just love to dream of the day that I can look up the aisle and see you coming toward me all dressed in white. Then we can go back up the aisle together as husband and wife. I know that you will be the most beautiful bride in the world — because you will be mine.

My wedding dress had a long wedding veil and long train. When Daddy and I started up the aisle, either the veil or the train (not sure which) hung on one of the back pews. I reached back and got it loose only to have it snag a second time! I was getting concerned.

Daddy was a nervous wreck; he told me later that he was about to rip the veil off my head and say,

"Get on down there and let's get this wedding DONE!"

Wedding Dress

Daddy's nervousness leads me to a funny memory! I was going to sing to Bill during the ceremony. After the exchange of rings, I wanted to sing a song called, "It Seems I've Always Loved You," by Ralph Carmichael. I had heard the song on an Oral Roberts' television special just a year before I met Bill. The song touched my heart so much that I ordered an album and a songbook with that song; I knew that someday I wanted to sing that at my wedding. Daddy was afraid that I would mess up the song and be horrified during the ceremony; he has always been nervous enough for the both of us! He gave me a "nerve pill" that the doctor had once prescribed for him. Neither of us knew how it was going to affect me, but just let me say that by the time I was heading down the aisle, I was feeling NO PAIN! Later on, Bill said that I was as high as a kite! LOL!

I stood at the back of the church and looked at the bridesmaids, at Bill, his daddy who was the best man, and the ushers, and I thought, "Well, here we are — all dressed up!" I thought it was hilarious! I almost laughed out loud, but the pastor had warned us during our premarital counseling session that couples are highly emotional during their weddings, and if they start laughing or crying, they may not be able to stop. I did have enough presence of mind to remember that warning, so I refrained from laughing as Daddy walked me down the aisle. Thank GOD!

During rehearsal, Bill and I stood and faced each other for the song. We were going to hold hands while I sang. I did not sing the song during the rehearsal because I wanted the words to be new for him. In order to help with my nerves, I did tell him that I planned to look slightly to his left when I sang to avoid looking into those beautiful eyes of his. I knew that my knees might buckle and the tears might start. He understood my concerns.

Well, it didn't turn out exactly like that. The "nerve" pill did its job! I still don't know exactly what DRUG I was on, but I wasn't nervous at all! I looked Bill dead in the eyes while I sang! I even winked at him! He was blown away! After we drove away from the church, he said, "Woman, I thought you were going to be nervous! What was that sassy wink about?" When I told him about the nerve pill, he nearly collapsed laughing. That's when he told me I was "high." I would not recommend taking ANY new medication before one's wedding; what if I have fallen asleep during the candle lighting ceremony! LOL! Thankfully, it just lifted my spirits a bit and took the edge off. I sang the song; we were pronounced man and wife, and we walked down the aisle together smiling from ear to ear.

Even though I may have needed a bit of "help" to get through it, I am so glad I mustered the nerve to sing the song. In retrospect it was the perfect song for our wedding. God knew what we would face, and I believe it was His Spirit that prompted me to order the music and decide to sing it on our wedding day.

After the reception, we changed clothes and jumped into Jezebel! I will never forget the exhilaration of driving away as a married couple! We were LEGAL! We had no money for a fancy honeymoon. Bill reserved two nights at a Holiday Inn in Roanoke and one night at a Howard Johnson's in Charlotte, North Carolina. The Holiday Inn was a little over $20 a night and the Howard Johnson's was a bargain at $18! Those prices are hilarious now, but we were absolutely dirt poor! I think that my wedding night may have been the very first night that I ever spent in a hotel! I don't remember ever staying in one before that. I did not care that the hotels were not expensive; I only cared that I was going to be with the man I loved. Nothing else mattered.

I'm not sure what time we got to the hotel in Roanoke, but it was getting close to suppertime. Bill had seen a restaurant close by and suggested we get something to eat there. Our wedding was in the middle of the afternoon, and it had been a long time since lunch. That little bite of cake and sip of punch at the reception were long gone! I had promised Mama that I would call her and let her know where we were. We'd kept our destination a secret because we didn't want family or friends showing up at the hotel to prank us! I called her from the hotel room before we left for supper. I was so happy and upbeat as I gave her the hotel name.

"Have you DONE IT yet?"

Yep! That's what my sweet mama *whispered* into the phone. Mama was only thirty-seven years old when I got married! Growing up, I could talk to Mama about anything; many of my friends told me they were jealous of our relationship because they didn't feel that freedom with their own moms. We had talked about my upcoming marriage many times during the past year. Mama and Daddy enjoyed each other; we grew up seeing them flirt with lots of kisses and giggles! She wanted me to have a good attitude about my love life with Bill. What a GIFT to have a mom like that! I am incredibly thankful for the advice she gave me, and the wonderful discussions we had.

"Mama, it's not even DARK yet!"

I laugh now when I remember that response. Some would wonder why Bill wanted us to eat supper first. After so many months of intense longing for each other, supper could have waited a bit! I suppose he was trying to be a gentleman, and maybe he was waiting for some sort of signal from me. I was simply following his lead. I ended the call with Mama, and Bill and I went for a nice supper. I'd love to be able to go back and be a fly on the wall during that meal. We were so deliriously happy— so much in love!

Bill had bought a beautiful negligee for me for our honeymoon. I took my time putting it on and preparing myself for this special moment while he waited patiently for me. Our wedding night was truly a sacred time for us. We came together as husband and wife, and it was beautiful. He was a tender lover, and he delighted in loving me. No woman could ever ask for more. We slept a bit late on Sunday morning and were enjoying some snuggles when two maids knocked on the door. I suppose we didn't know to put out the "Do Not Disturb" sign on the door; I'm not sure we even had one of those back then.

Bill said, ***"We are still here."***

One of the maids said to the other, "***Well, they can't stay in bed ALL DAY!"***

Bill reached out and grabbed me as he said, ***"Just watch US!"***

Well, we didn't stay in bed ALL day. Eventually, we got up and went to a doughnut shop we had seen. Bill bought a few doughnuts and something to drink — neither of us drank coffee back then. We drove Jezebel up to the Parkway and found a beautiful overlook. The back of the Rambler (a station wagon) was filled with presents from the wedding. We unwrapped each one as we enjoyed the doughnuts.

After that, we drove back to the hotel for some more LOVIN! Well, it was our honeymoon!

Our third night as husband and wife was spent in Charlotte where Bill bought tickets for a new amusement park called Carowinds. We enjoyed a day there before heading on to Georgia. He drove through Cherokee, North Carolina, because I had never been there. Not having enough money for another hotel stay, we just drove through and stopped at a couple of tourist shops along the way.

Honeymoon in Cherokee

We were both anxious to get to our little basement apartment in Franklin Springs and begin our married life together. When I look back at our honeymoon, I don't remember the small details about the rooms or the places we visited. I remember the absolute delight we took in each other. I remember the pure joy of learning how to love each other, the sacredness of that intimacy. We were so happy we could barely contain ourselves. There is nothing in this world that could ever replace the wonder of those few days. The journey ahead would not be an easy one for us, and we had no idea what was coming. All we knew was that our love was true. God had placed us together; we felt a sense of destiny that was special.

That foundation often sustained us when nothing else would.

Chapter Ten

Franklin Springs Part I

Letter from Karen July 22, 1973

… most of all you make me feel loved and wanted. I trust you and I know that I'll be happy with you. Adjusting to married life will be difficult at first, but that's to be expected. We'll just have to have faith in God and each other, and love for God and each other. It's hard for me to imagine myself married, but yet I can and do picture myself as your wife, companion, lover, and friend. I love myself in that role. I want so badly to make you happy.

Adjusting to married life is something each couple must do. No matter how great the lovemaking is, and it ***IS*** pretty ***GREAT***, day-to-day living is something else entirely. It is a good thing that most couples are young and passionate when they do marry because that provides a great cushion for the lack of money and stresses of real life! God provided a safe haven for our early married years when he gave us our first small apartment.

When we were planning our wedding during our sophomore year, we knew we needed a place to live. Many folks in Franklin County had small apartments in their homes or above their garages which they rented to college students. We found out that Rev. and Mrs. Walt Crawford had a basement apartment that was going to be available after our wedding, so we spoke to them about it and went to see it.

It was a basement apartment, so yes, it smelled like mildew most of the time! They used a dehumidifier, but Georgia's humidity is the stuff of nightmares; it cannot be denied! We could enter the apartment from the carport. There was a narrow hallway straight down the apartment from the carport door. The kitchen (very tiny) and the living room (a decent size) were on the right upon entering. The only true bedroom was at the far end beside the living room. The hallway from the bedroom to the carport was narrow, and we could see the carport door from our bedroom door; it was a straight shot (remember that). There was one small bath (walk-in shower, no tub), one small closet, and another narrow space with the hot water heater in it. All three of these spaces were on the left side of the narrow hallway. There was a stairway from the hallway that went upstairs to the main floor of the house.

Oak Dining Table

We lived there for two years. It was fully furnished, but Bill and I did purchase a 19" black and white television right away and a solid oak dining table a few months later with six caned chairs. That oak dining set is still in my kitchen today. We had to buy it on an installment plan, and it was a huge purchase for us. It has been in every place we have ever lived. On many occasions I hinted that we should buy a more updated table, but Bill always had a response.

"We bought a GOOD table! It's STILL a GOOD table!"

Bill's Closet "Office"

He was right. It is a good table, and the memories we made around it are priceless. Bill turned the little hall closet into his "study." He put a small desk inside and sat a small bookcase on top of the desk. He could leave the door open and sit halfway in the hallway to read, study, and write for his college classes. I have a precious photo of him doing just that. We even put a set of bunkbeds into the water heater closet! There was barely enough room to get into and out of the beds, but if we had visitors, they were welcome to TRY to sleep there.

Ma and Dad Crawford — what a pair they were!

The Crawford's home was a beautiful brick home that sat on a hilltop just outside of Franklin Springs, Georgia. All of the students called them "Ma and Dad." They were transplanted Canadians who dearly loved the college students. Bill and I met them for the first time when we came to Emmanuel, but we had known about Walt Crawford all of our lives.

Dad Crawford painted pictures for the Sunday School literature of the Pentecostal Holiness Church (now known as the International Pentecostal Holiness Church or IPHC). We grew up looking at his pictures in our Sunday School books each week! His beautiful paintings also hung in many of our churches across the United States. Both of us knew his name well, but we had never met him in person until we came to Emmanuel in 1972. Ma worked in the college canteen, and her personality was amazing! Everybody loved Ma! She was bold and boisterous — definitely not like the "refined" little southern ladies we were accustomed to. She was funny and so easy to love.

Here is my favorite "Ma" story. Back in "tha day" I enjoyed sunbathing before I knew how it would damage my skin. I wanted to lie in the sun after we got married, but I didn't know if Ma and Dad would approve. Bill advised me just to check with Ma and see what she would think. NEVER in a million years did I expect our conversation to go like this:

> Me: ***"Ma, would it be alright for me to lie out in the sun a little in the back yard? I will only do it when no one is here, and no one can see in that part of the backyard because of all the trees. (There also weren't any other houses close enough to see anything.)***
>
> Ma: ***"Sure! Absolutely! You really should sunbathe in the nude! Bill would just LOVE it if you were tanned ALL OVER!"***
>
> Me:

Needless to say, I had NO WORDS! Eventually I stumbled through something like

> ***"That's okay. I have a nice bathing suit which will be fine. Thanks, Ma!"***

When I told Bill what she said, he was eating something and nearly choked to death! After he got through choking, we both laughed until we couldn't laugh anymore! Just hearing that from sweet little "Ma" was more than we could handle.

I cannot count the times that she would knock on the stairway door, stick her head in and yell to us.

> ***"Have you guys eaten yet (in her Yankee accent)? I have some ___ if you want some!"***

Whatever it was, it was good! We enjoyed many leftovers from their meals. They were watching out for us and taking good care of us. They knew we had no money; they knew it was a struggle. God gave them to us for two wonderful years, and what a blessing they were!

A bit of unwelcome excitement occurred the first morning after we arrived from our honeymoon. We were thrilled to be settling into our first little "home," and we were still enjoying a honeymoon atmosphere! We had slept in a bit and were enjoying some "quality" time. The bedroom door was NOT completely shut, and suddenly we heard the apartment door open and someone walking down the hallway — right towards us!

Bill jumped up — NOT dressed — and slammed the door shut and LOCKED it!

> ***"Who is it?"*** he yelled!

I don't remember who it was now, but Dad and Ma had not expected us to return from our honeymoon that quickly. They had some repair person coming in to check something before we arrived. They had given him a key to use which he was going to return after the work. He was able to do whatever needed to be done, and he had not SEEN anything. Whew! That was a close one!

One of my sweetest memories is when I cooked our first breakfast in the apartment. Bill offered to help, but I was determined to show him that I could at least scramble eggs! It was probably the SAME day that we had the unexpected visitor, but I can't remember for sure. It was such fun to pull out some of our new dishes and place them on the furnished metal table. I wanted everything to look nice! I scrambled some eggs, made grits (for the first time) and buttered some toast. Everything looked okay, and I fixed our plates. After Bill prayed a blessing, I took a bite. Oh my, it was pretty bad! I had not grown up eating grits with butter and salt; we ate them with milk and sugar. Don't hold that against me! My grits were too runny, and the scrambled eggs had a slightly scorched taste. I glanced over at Bill, and he was dutifully taking small bites without making eye contact with me. BLESS HIS HEART! He was going to eat that nasty breakfast and not say one word. Seeing him doing that just made me love him even more!

I reached over and put my hand on his arm.

"Honey, you don't have to eat this. I'm sorry. It's pretty awful."

He paused. He didn't say anything for a few seconds. I'm sure he was weighing several scenarios in his mind without knowing what the possible consequences might be! This was dangerous and unknown terrain for a man newly married!

Finally, with hesitation he said, ***"Are you sure?"***

I replied, ***"Yes, I am sure. I tried, but this is pretty bad."***

He smiled, got up, and took our plates to the kitchen. He scraped everything into the garbage and proceeded to cook up a delicious breakfast for us! He enjoyed cooking and never minded fixing a meal. I'm still not a great cook, and I don't particularly enjoy cooking. I like to bake, and I can follow most recipes, but anything I really know about the kitchen, Bill taught me.

After we had eaten, he wrapped his long arms around me and reminded me again that he had ***NOT*** married me to be his cook. How I loved that man!

Chapter Eleven

Franklin Springs Part II

Those first two years of marriage were filled with new beginnings which included more than Bill's adjustments to my lack of culinary skill. He received his license to preach the first week we were back in Franklin Springs. The annual campmeeting services were being held in the old college gymtorium. We blushed at all the smiles and smirks we received when we walked into the services as man and wife. We loved it! We found our niche in the Franklin Springs Pentecostal Holiness Church as a married couple. Each "first" was a new adventure and part of the early marriage experience.

Griffins visit apartment

I remember how excited we became when we found out that Paula and Billy were coming to visit us! It would be our first time to host friends in our little apartment! On their first morning, we woke up early to start getting breakfast ready for them. I was learning to be Bill's sous chef; I followed his lead and just did what he said. It suited Bill perfectly and was the pattern we would follow for the rest of our marriage. When I put my feet on the floor, I stepped into a couple of inches of WATER! We had been experiencing a lot of rain in Georgia, and the basement had flooded a bit. Have Mercy! It was worse in the back bedroom than anywhere else, but we knew we needed to act fast! Dad had a wet vac, and he helped all four of us get that water out very quickly. It was a little more excitement than we had planned for, but thankfully no real damage was done.

Ma and Dad were wonderful blessings to us. We had not lived with them very long when Dad told us that he was going to REDUCE our rent. He felt that he was supposed to do that. The Crawfords were very in tune with God's Spirit; they inspired everyone they knew with their spiritual walk. One night during our second year there, Dad yelled down the steps and asked us to come up to his art studio.

Walt Crawford's Jesus

He was working on a painting of Jesus. He told us that he wanted a bit more of a modern look for Jesus, and he wanted a more masculine Jesus. We enjoyed being in the studio with this talented man and seeing him work. He wanted our opinions on the painting. We loved it! After a few minutes of talking, Dad said he wanted to pray for us before we left. He was in the middle of praying a nice prayer when he just stopped.

"God is going to give you a son."

That is what he said. He paused a few seconds and ended the prayer. There was no further explanation; nothing else was said about THAT.

We had only been married a little over a year. I was taking birth control pills at the time; we were not trying to get pregnant, and we really didn't think we would have any trouble. Surely, God would bless us and give us children; we were going into the ministry! We still thought it was a sure thing. It was nice that Dad would say that in his prayer, but we did not place the importance on that moment that it deserved. We really had no full understanding of what had just happened.

Dad Crawford was the very first to prophesy over us about a child. There would be several other prophecies to come, but Dad's was always extra special because his was the first, and it was specifically about a SON.

Decades later, long after both Ma and Dad had gone to Heaven, Bill received an interesting phone call. I am not sure about all of the details, but a certain painting of Dad's was going to be purchased, and the buyer had not come to pick it up. Someone thought of us and called Bill to see if we would like it. There were actually TWO paintings in the parcel. Guess what! When Bill brought them home, the painting of Jesus was one of them! Isn't that just like God! We had never even considered such a thing, and now the painting that intrigued us on the night the FIRST prophecy of our son was given was OURS! It hangs in our home today. What a generous and loving God we serve!

The one BIG fly in the ointment during the first two years of our marriage is that I had to put my education on hold. There was simply no way that we could afford for me to go to school while Bill finished his undergraduate degree. My parents were not happy, and neither were we, but there was no other way. I promised Daddy that I would eventually go back to school and get my degree, but I'm not sure he believed me. Many other young women had the same dreams, but pregnancies or finances would get in the way.

I got a job at a new Westclox factory which had been built right across the road from the college. Bill would be in classes while I worked at Westclox. He dropped me off in the morning and picked me up after work since the only vehicle we owned was Jezebel. I trained to inspect pocket watches at the end of an assembly line. It was probably the worst job I ever had, and I believe God used it to enforce my desire to complete my degree!

It took me less than ten seconds to do my inspection. I sat near the end of a row of women facing straight ahead, as the assembly line passed on my right. The watches were placed about 12-14" apart. For eight LONG hours, the watches would come. I would pick one up, check-check-check-check-check, place the inspected watch back on the line and pick up the next. If we got a bad "run" of watches, there would be problems which I was expected to see. I would write a certain number on the watch mechanism (the hands, the case, and the crystal were placed after the inspection) and set it aside. During breaks, I would see if I could repair the problem. If not, the rejects had to go to a different repair station.

All of the workers on the line were women. Smaller hands/fingers made the work easier; women could do the job faster, and speed was everything on the assembly line. Most of you have seen the Lucy and Ethel scene with the chocolates on the assembly line. At least they could EAT their work! We often felt the pressure that they felt, but we couldn't eat the pocket watches! Most (if not all) of the corporate managers were men. I resented that women did the work, but the men wanted to tell us HOW to do it. I am not and have never considered myself a feminist, but I chafed under that particular system. On more than one occasion I spoke out about what I saw as an unfair policy or decision. Most of the women on the line would complain, but they would not speak up. I could have been fired, but I wasn't willing to be silent. I'm sure Westclox was glad when I moved on! I know that I was!

I had often wondered if I really wanted to go into education, but those two years at Westclox definitely silenced every doubt! I knew that I needed a career that allowed me to be at least a little creative. I wanted to be able to look out the windows from time to time (the factory did NOT have windows in the work areas). I NEEDED to be able to TALK; I suppose that's a true character trait for teachers! Most of our report cards had "Talks too much" written on them at some point in our histories! I placed a small two-year calendar card on my workstation, and I circled a day in June of 1976 when I assumed Bill would graduate; I didn't know the exact date yet. I marked off every single day for two years! I seriously hated that job, and his graduation could not come soon enough for me!

During Bill's senior year the monotony of the job was really getting to me. It took me about eight seconds to do my inspection — EIGHT SECONDS! I did it over and over and over for eight LONG hours each day! I could just about do the inspection with my eyes closed, and I started daydreaming about what Bill might be doing. I would imagine him sitting in class with cute girls and laughing all day! I would picture him grabbing a bite to eat with cute girls (ALWAYS cute girls) and having interesting and stimulating conversations while I sat at that assembly line, wearing my safety glasses with a jeweler's loop to see inside the watches. I was not a pretty sight; I can assure you of that! Bill would come to pick me up at 5:00 when I got off my shift.

"Hey Babe! Did you have a good day?"

"No, I did NOT have a good Day! How was YOUR day????"

We would laugh about it later on, but I'd be mad at the poor guy, and he had not done a single thing! I was mad at what I had IMAGINED he had done. I think Bill was happier than I was when I could finally walk out of Westclox for the last time!

Those early years were lean years financially; they usually are for most married couples. I always did what I could to save money throughout our marriage, but especially when money was tight. My mama always cut her own hair and made most of our clothes when I was growing up. In the fourth grade, I decided that I could cut my own hair, and Mama gave me permission to do so! Needless to say, I have survived many horrific haircuts, but at least they were FREE! I also made many of my clothes and lots of curtains and costumes (church plays and school programs) over the years.

Right before our first anniversary in 1975, women were beginning to use home high-lighting kits. I decided to try that for myself. I was very cautious and tried to just get a few thin highlights around my face. It was on a Sunday afternoon, and Bill was going to be gone for a few hours; my plan was to surprise him. Boy! Did I ever surprise him! After I'd rinsed and dried my hair, I was disappointed because I could barely see the new highlights at all! I decided to try one more time. This time I REALLY put on the product! I made larger highlights and more of them and processed a bit longer; I was so proud of myself! I could hardly wait to see the NEW and BEAUTIFUL me in the mirror!

When I rinsed and began to dry my hair in our little apartment bathroom, I was absolutely mortified to see the LARGE YELLOW blobs in my hair! I mean NEON YELLOW! I knew nothing about toning, and I don't even remember having any toner in the box. It was like the Bride of Frankenstein looking back at me! I fell down on the bathroom floor and sobbed! I could NOT let Bill see me like THIS!

I didn't know what to do! There weren't many stores open late on a Sunday afternoon in the Franklin Springs/Royston area in 1975! I found a small pharmacy that had a few boxes of hair color. Unfortunately, they were only temporary hair colors; I'd have to wait a few days before I could purchase a permanent hair color. I chose a brown close to my natural color and rushed home. I had no idea if it would cover the NEON YELLOW or not, but I had to do something.

I grabbed the scissors and cut my hair as short as it had ever been at that point! I thought the drastic haircut might minimize the COLOR disaster! In the poor bathroom lighting, the color looked "almost" okay; it was certainly better than the yellow stripes in my hair. I worked at styling the short cut and thought I was presentable when Bill came home and greeted me at the door.

"You cut your hair!"

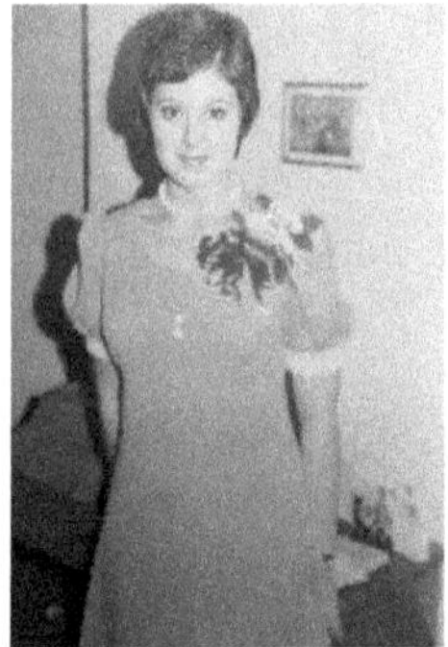

Post-Hair Disaster

Thankfully, he was not too shocked. He knew that I cut my own hair, and he never was a guy who preferred long hair on women. He liked me with short hair, so he wasn't turned off by it. He was surprised because I had not talked about cutting my hair. He said the color looked a bit different, and I dismissed his concerns. I did NOT tell him what I had done; I knew he would have a fit about the highlight disaster!

The next day at Westclox, I found out how BAD my hair color solution truly was. It was a pretty day, so several of us took our lunch break outside. We were talking and eating our sandwiches when one of my friends looked at me strangely and said,

"Karen, your hair looks GREEN today!"

I just laughed it off without any explanation and quickly went back inside where the light was NOT so bright! I did not tell anyone about my ridiculous highlighting experience! I bought a better quality, permanent hair color after work that day and used it before my next hair wash. I waited awhile before I told Bill what I had done. He told me NEVER to do anything like that AGAIN! He was concerned with all the processing (two rounds of highlights, semi-permanent color, and permanent color), my hair might fall out! Over the years, I have cut my own hair, colored my hair, highlighted my hair, straightened my hair, and given myself perms, but I have been more careful and tried to avoid another hair "disaster." I think I've gone to a salon less than ten times in my adult life.

Yes, I have lived through some pretty bad hairstyles, but most of us have! I have certainly saved a lot of money by doing it myself. That pleased the BUDGET KING, and I think a little bit of his financial management rubbed off on me over the years. I do like nice things, but I am always on the hunt for a BARGAIN!

Those two years in Franklin Springs- other than the job at Westclox- were really good for us in many ways. I am thankful that the pay was pretty good at my job; we really needed the money. We learned a lot about each other during those early years of marriage. We enjoyed loving each other. Driving to Hartwell to buy groceries on Friday evenings and grabbing a burger at the local Dairy Queen was our idea of "date night." Cuddling up on the green fold-out couch in our basement living room and watching television on our little 19" television was fun. We often took advantage of that little fold-out couch as well, and we weren't always watching television! We were young and crazy in love with each other. My job was horrible, and we still had no extra money, but we lived on LOVE, and it was absolutely delicious!

One night we were just enjoying some snuggles as we began to dose off. Bill was lying on his stomach, and I was gently rubbing his back as I began to slip in and out of light sleep. Suddenly, I felt something strange. I quickly became alert, and fear gripped me. I could not figure out what it was; it was too large to be a pimple! Was it a boil, a cyst, or a tumor of some kind! I began to feel around it and try to figure it out in the dark.

Bill asked, ***"Woman, what ARE you doing?"***

I responded, ***"Honey, there is something AWFUL on your back! I'm scared! Turn on the light NOW!***

"Have mercy, Girl! I rolled over; that's my NIPPLE!"

We dissolved into laughter as he took me in his arms and held me to his broad chest. He laughed as he held me; I could feel his breath blowing the hair on the top of my head. I will never forget just the sheer joy of that silly moment. We laughed about that for the rest of our marriage, and I'm laughing right now as I type this. We laughed a lot in our marriage. It was harder during the difficult times, but as long as Bill could keep me laughing, he could keep me looking up.

> ***"Being cheerful keeps you healthy. It is slow death to be gloomy all the time."*** **(Proverbs 17:22 Good News Translation)**

Bill graduated with his bachelor's degree in June 1976. Our time in Franklin Springs had come to an end. The next two years would hold new challenges and new rewards, and we hoped we were ready for them. Time to move to GRIFFIN!

Chapter Twelve

Griffin

Bill was now a fully ordained minister with a college degree. WhooHoo! I could quit Westclox and get back to the business of earning my own degree! We were both excited at the path that lay before us. He had been serving as an intern pastor at a church in Athens, Georgia, during his senior year at Emmanuel. The pastor had told us that he wanted us to stay there. Bill would become a full-time assistant pastor while I attended the University of Georgia. The church had bought new property which had a small frame house on it where we could live as part of Bill's employment package. I applied to the University, was accepted, and even attended an orientation for new students. Things took an unexpected turn when the church board decided that the plans for building a new church would take more funds than they had originally thought. Hiring a new full-time assistant might be too big of a risk for the growing congregation. They decided that they could not hire Bill at that time.

I won't lie; we were terribly disappointed. The original plan seemed like such a good one, and we adored the folks in that congregation and enjoyed working with the pastor. These things happen, though, so we started praying earnestly for God to open a door. Our conference superintendent asked Bill to go and preach at a little church in Griffin. We didn't know what to expect when we arrived, but to say that this was a challenging situation would be an understatement.

Griffin Church

The church building itself had been a Methodist church at one time. It seemed skinny and tall from the front. It was located in a run-down section of town with a Salvation Army one block over. There was a cotton mill across the nearby railroad track, and most of the houses near the church had been part of a mill village many years ago. The little parsonage was right beside the church; only a narrow driveway separated the two buildings. Neither the church nor the parsonage had air conditioning, and Griffin gets VERY hot in the summer! We soon discovered that the tall church also blocked any breezes from that side — not a good thing! We visited there on a Sunday morning, and the congregation was quite slim. I don't remember how many were there, but probably 15-25 at the most. We met a few of the folks, and they were friendly but didn't seem to have much hope. This tugged at our hearts.

I say all of that to say this: there was NOTHING in Griffin that would make us want to go there, to live there, to pastor that church. Nothing in the physical was attractive, but something in the spiritual spoke to us. When we left there and drove the two and a half hours it took to get back to Franklin Springs, we had a long talk about the Griffin church. We both felt a pull, and we knew that God was leading us. It was a bit scary to take on such an undertaking, and we really didn't know how tough it would be. We were just sensing the leading of the Holy Spirit and trying to be obedient. It is also important to remember that we were both only twenty-one years old at the time. I am thankful that we were willing to take that risk. Many pastors today are unwilling to go into a difficult situation and grow a church. Bill was always willing to take the risk. My man was brave. He never backed down from a challenge or walked away from a fight that needed fighting.

We accepted that church and moved to Griffin. Our first Sunday night service with Bill as pastor had five people present — counting the two of us! Yep! You read that right! Sunday mornings would range between twenty and thirty people in the beginning. We learned that most of the congregation lived in other neighborhoods and did not want to drive back to the church for a Sunday night service.

Griffin Parsonage

The church did clean up the little parsonage; they had been renting it to some guy with a motorcycle. It was not in good condition, and there were motorcycle skid marks on the front porch that we could never get off! They put new kitchen cabinets and a new kitchen floor in before we moved which was a huge blessing! They cleaned everything the best they could, and we greatly appreciated that. They welcomed us with open arms and seemed genuinely thankful that we were there.

We had a bit of a scare the first week after we had moved in. We learned that someone had pulled a knife on a woman in front of the church not long before we came. That was a bit unsettling, especially for me. Knowing about that particular incident only added to the fear that we encountered on one of those first nights in the house. We were sitting in the den watching television. The window was open because it was a warm night. Suddenly we heard loud noises and LOTS of cursing! It sounded like a gang was in our backyard! The parsonage was just a few feet away from the church, and there was no separation between our backyards. I was terrified! Bill — being Bill — said he was going out to see what was going on! I begged him to call the police instead because he had no idea what he was walking into. He said it was church property, and he was responsible for it. I PRAYED as he took a flashlight and walked out the back door to see what was going on.

Things finally got quiet, and I had no idea whether he was alive or dead! My heart was racing as he walked in the back door with a sheepish grin on his face.

> ***"What in the world happened out there?"***
>
> He smiled and said, "***Relax Honey, they were all kids. They looked like they were ten-twelve years old! They didn't know that we had moved in, and they didn't know that I am the pastor here. They told me that they had been settling their differences (fighting) behind the church for quite a while. I told them they could not do that any longer, and they said they wouldn't. I also invited them to come to church!"***

After hearing the CUSSIN' that those kids could do, I still wasn't convinced. Bill just laughed at me and did his best to get my mind on "other" things. I will say that he was pretty good at doing just that! When he walked out that back door, he did not know that they were so young. Their voices did NOT sound young. He walked out that back door and could have been walking into something very dangerous. That may have been the first time I saw the courage in Bill Jones, but it wouldn't be the last.

Bill made $50 a week for those two years. We found out that Tift College, a woman's Christian college was only about thirty miles away in Forsyth. It was an easy drive through the country to get there which sounded great to me. I had been concerned that I would have to find a college in the Atlanta area and commute there. Tift College of Education is now part of Mercer University. Tift was a smaller college, and my experience there was wonderful! I felt right at home after studying at Emmanuel for two years, and it didn't bother me that there were no male students. I was married and had my own MAN at home now!

Bill did not ask me to work a job while attending Tift. He knew that my classwork plus the commute would make it difficult for me to hold down a job as well. He did some substitute teaching to help make ends meet, but those Griffin years were LEAN years. There were times when we had no money for groceries! We didn't have Ma Crawford asking if we wanted leftovers either, but God provided. In those days, I wore skirts and pantyhose to class. I would buy Today's Girl pantyhose for .99 at

K-Mart. We were so poor that I'd have to ask Bill if I could have a dollar to buy some new hose! I would put fingernail polish on the runs until I felt like all I was wearing was one big RUN! Young folks won't understand that illustration at all, but those of you with a few wrinkles on your forehead should.

During one particularly lean time, we were getting concerned. The cupboards were getting bare, and Bill had not been called to substitute in a while. We didn't have credit cards back then, so if we didn't have a dollar; we did NOT have a dollar! I came home from classes one day and found two or three large bags of groceries on the front porch! Praise God! We never did know where they came from; we had not spoken about our predicament to anyone. God saw our need and met it! To say we were happy is an understatement for sure.

At one point we owed a big bill for something. I can't remember what it was, and the amount may not seem like much today. It may have been something like $175 dollars, but it may as well have been $175,000 dollars! We did not have the money, and we had no way to get the money. That would have been nearly a month's salary for Bill if we had no other bills to pay! We were quite concerned and had prayed for God to help us. We did not want to ask our parents for money either. They were still struggling financially themselves, plus we did not want them to think that we could not take care of ourselves. We had chosen to push ahead and get married at nineteen, and we did not want to admit that we were struggling.

Just a day or two before the bill was due, two letters came in the mail. Both letters were from people we had not seen in a year or more. We had not communicated with either of these families; the letters were just OUT OF THE BLUE, and they arrived the same day! Both letters wanted to know how we were doing. They both said that we had been on their hearts, and they both said they had felt led to send us a small gift. Both letters contained checks. The two checks together were the EXACT amount that we owed on the upcoming bill! We cried as we sat together and saw the hand of God working on our behalf. Those times were difficult, but God was proving Himself to us. He SAW us; He KNEW what we were facing, and He was seeing that our needs were met. We didn't have everything we wanted, but He was providing our needs.

Those lessons learned in Griffin stayed with us for our entire ministry. God is faithful. He SEES us; He hears our prayers; He provides. Praise His wonderful name!

Bill began to gather neighborhood kids on the empty lot across from the church. He would play ball with them. We put a ping pong table in the backyard behind the parsonage and would play ping pong with the kids. Before long we had a pretty good group of children and young people attending church and a few of their parents. There were some parents that we never could get to commit, but the ones who did became faithful church members. When we left in 1978 the church was running consistently in the sixties. It wasn't what we wanted, but it was a start. Bill had big plans for the church.

Tift Graduation

I graduated Tift College magna cum laude in June of 1978. I had done my student teaching at the large Griffin High School and had been offered a job there for the fall of 1978. Bill had plans for the church to buy property on a better side of town. He and I would buy a trailer for us to live in until the church could build a new church on the property. The existing parsonage could then be used as more space for the growing church. He turned on his financial planning mode and had everything planned out for a presentation to the church. I was so proud of him, and we were very excited about what was ahead!

Unfortunately, a good number of those in leadership did not agree. None of the church leadership lived in the neighborhood where the church was located, and yet some of them did not want the church to relocate. At that time our churches voted on the pastors every two years. That was something that carried over from our Methodist roots. When Bill and I went through that first voting experience, we were naïve. We could see how the church had grown. We thought they loved us! We never expected that many would vote against us. I know now that they weren't voting against US as much as they were voting against Bill's plans to grow and expand even more. It would not be the last time that a church board would not be in agreement with Bill's vision. Each time was horribly painful and terribly disappointing for us.

We could have stayed in Griffin; the vote was truly not that bad, but Bill was disillusioned by it. He did not want to stay there and be forced to continue in a neighborhood that was becoming increasingly dangerous. In many ways, we felt like we had failed the Griffin church. Over the years we saw much fruit come from our years there. We saw folks who had gotten saved under our ministry continue to serve God and reach others. We saw some of those young people go into ministry themselves! David Hammond, a young boy who brought his little brothers and sisters to church, grew up to become a pastor and worked as Bill's associate in conference leadership. What a blessing!

Sometimes ministry may not appear to be successful. Every pastor doesn't have a mega-church! Every singer doesn't win a Dove Award. God sees ministry differently. I know we were obedient to God's call in going to Griffin. God did not hold us accountable for those who did not want to move. We planted seed there for as long as we could; we did our best to be obedient to the Call. When Bill felt that season was over, he reached out to our conference leadership for direction. He was a man who valued authority, and he always believed in working under authority. He asked the conference board to pray and seek God for direction for us.

There were a couple of churches that were going to be open. One was in Elberton, and one was in the Atlanta area. Elberton was a small town built on the granite industry. It had a reputation of being a hard place to minister; some said it was as hard as the granite it sat on! The church near Atlanta was not a big church, but the potential for growth there was impressive. The conference board told Bill he could choose, and most folks would have assumed that the Atlanta-area church would be the obvious choice. Bill refused to decide; he told the board that he had agreed to operate under their authority. He believed God would work through them, and He did. We all prayed, and the board decided to send us to Elberton.

We felt good about it; we had peace. It was the right move for us, but it would NOT be an easy ministry. So many things were waiting for us in Elberton. Some of our biggest miracles were waiting for us there, but we were also getting ready to meet some earth-shattering and life-threatening obstacles. Writing about some of those things is going to be difficult.

May God direct me and help me to share honestly. You cannot appreciate the miracles until you fully understand the heartache that went before them.

Chapter Thirteen

Elberton

Moving to Elberton was exciting! We were heading back to the northeast Georgia area, and we loved it! We were only thirty minutes from Emmanuel and many of our old friends. Thirty-five minutes in another direction would take us to Athens where we had even more friends. It also placed us a good two hours closer to our families in Virginia and North Carolina which was great for them as well.

We had lived in Griffin for two years, and I never ran into anyone I knew outside of the church. The town was big enough and the church was small enough that the odds were against it. Elberton was smaller than Griffin, and the church had a bigger congregation. I also started my teaching career there, so I met more local people. It seemed as if everywhere I went, I ran into someone I knew! I found that comforting. The church in Elberton was a solid church with a good congregation. The parsonage was still located beside the church, but it was a much larger frame house, and it had air conditioning! Thank You, Jesus! We had a good-sized kitchen, a nice living room

Preaching in Elberton

and dining room, plus three bedrooms and two baths. There was also an upstairs which we used for storage.

1st year Teacher

The first few years were exciting. I made great friends teaching at the local middle school. The church grew, and we experienced a wonderful season of revival. Bill was maturing in his ministry and gaining more confidence than ever. After I started teaching school, the finances eased up a bit. Bill was earning a better salary as well. We bought more furniture which we desperately needed, and we bought a new car. Jezebel had given up the ghost, and we needed a dependable car. One of our church members owned a local car dealership, and he helped us buy our first NEW car. We were so thankful! We were even able to afford a short vacation to Florida, and we drove there in our new car. What a thrill! Life was good!

After getting a little more financially stable, we decided to start trying to get pregnant. We both thought that it would happen soon. We had absolutely NO difficulties in the TRYING department, so we assumed that success would come easily. It didn't. The first few months didn't concern us too much, but as we began to approach that one year mark, our resolve took a beating.

Florida Vacation

Without going into too much detail, we began to have tests run. They checked me first. They checked my ovaries; they checked me for endometriosis; they checked my hormone levels, and I can't remember what else. All of my tests came back fine. It seems strange to me that they would test ME first, when a sperm count is a much easier test to do. Why not check the MAN first? Maybe they do that now; I'm not sure. I also know that the insurance company paid a good amount of money to have those tests run on me. Ummm…maybe that is the reason they checked me first.

Bill's sperm count was low, but the biggest problem was motility. The doctor told us that it wasn't impossible for us to get pregnant, but it might not be easy. They were willing to try some different things, but Bill wasn't quite ready to attempt any of them at that point. I was comfortable with us just continuing to try a bit longer, so that is what we did. We just kept TRYING and enjoying every minute of it!

As month after month rolled by, I became more concerned. Infertility is hard on both men and women, but I do believe it is harder on the wife. We are created to carry babies in our wombs. Each and every month we are reminded when our pregnancy attempts fail. That pain in our ovaries or the stain on our clothes breaks our heart each month. Each and every month — after month — after month.

I would day dream about being able to announce our pregnancy to our family over Thanksgiving turkey or during Christmas as we opened presents under the Christmas tree. Every single time I was a day or two late, I would get excited about the possibility that I could tell Bill I was pregnant! Each time my hopes were dashed, my heart broke just a bit more. Now it was more about YEARS passing instead of months.

Even in modern times, women are looked down upon when they are infertile. It does not matter that the husband's sperm count may be low or nonexistent. Since women carry the babies; they are the ones who are seen as "flawed" to the world. I faced this even in the church. At almost every church service, someone wanted to lay lands on me and pray for me to have a baby. At one point I said to Bill, "The next person who comes at me wanting to lay hands on my stomach is going to get kicked into the next town!" I'd had it at that point. Enough was enough!

I once had a woman say to me, "All MY husband ever had to do was take his pants off, and I got pregnant!" It was a ladies' outing, and the others just laughed and laughed at that comment. I tried to smile, but I was dying inside. I didn't know if she was putting me down for NOT getting pregnant or Bill for not being ABLE to get me pregnant. Either way, it was insulting and unkind. Later on, I would get bolder and address those types of comments. Some things just need to be addressed; Bill taught me that! I had ladies start conversations where they were trying to ask me if Bill and I were "doing it" correctly. Yep! THAT! Well, I can assure you, we were DOING it correctly, and we were doing it OFTEN, but it just was not making a baby for us. How ridiculous was that? I could hardly believe what people were thinking or saying, and we were suffering in the middle of it. Not only were we doing ***IT***; we were doing everything but doing it upside down! The scheduling, the temperature taking, the loose underwear for Bill, almost standing me on my head…we did it ALL! Nothing worked, though. Nothing…

We had moved to Elberton in 1978. By the time Thanksgiving and Christmas rolled around in 1981 we were getting serious about having a baby and talked to the doctor about attempting something he had suggested. They would collect several sperm samples from Bill and make a sort of concentrate which would increase our odds. It was less invasive than other options, and it was worth a try!

We hoped to start the process after the holidays, but a new challenge was coming our way. This challenge would take baby-making off our radar for quite a while.

Chapter Fourteen

Dreams Dashed

Letter from Bill: August 22, 1973

I'm a little discouraged. I want to be a strong, well man for you. I want to make you happy and love you for a long time — not be sick with a kidney infection. But I am still determined to go on. God has called me to preach, and He has given me a beautiful woman to love, so I'm not about to give up. I'm gonna marry you next summer and love you just as long as I live. I love you, and I'm gonna love you forever. I'm even gonna marry you. Corroded kidneys or not. Pray for me. I love you very much, Baby.

Each Christmas we would make the long drives to Virginia and North Carolina. We would go to Virginia first because our family get together was traditionally on Christmas Eve. For many years we would get up on Christmas morning, open presents with my family, and then drive the five-six hours to Clinton for their gathering on Christmas night. Sometimes the schedule would change a little bit, but that's what we did most of the time.

On our drive to Virginia in 1981, I noticed that Bill's stomach was nearly touching the steering wheel! Bill was a big man; there is no denying that, but he had never had a big stomach. As a young man, he carried most of his weight in his broad shoulders. I mentioned it to him, and asked him how much weight he had gained. He said he had not been eating more, and he couldn't understand why his stomach was so enlarged. I told him we would have to start a serious diet after we got back home from the holidays.

During the Christmas travels, Bill got sick a couple of times, but it was easy to attribute it to eating too much at a meal or eating too many sweets. He just didn't feel well for most of the trip. He had a regular doctor's appointment already scheduled for a yearly check-up in January, so he decided to wait until then to see the doctor. Neither one of us thought it was anything serious.

We came back from the holidays, and I went back to my classroom. I taught in an older middle school at the time, and there was a huge bank of windows facing the main entrance to the school. Whenever Bill came by the school, he parked outside my room. Sometimes, he would just come up to the window and tell me something right there. I saw him drive up, but he parked and got out of the car. I knew he would be at my door in a matter of minutes, so I edged over so I'd be close by. The students were working quietly, so I knew I could step into the hall.

He looked serious, ***"Honey, I've got bad news."***

"From the doctor?"

"My kidney is failing. I've got to go to the hospital."

The world stopped turning. It were as if I became deaf; the silence was oppressive. Breathing was difficult. I truly didn't understand exactly what was happening, but our lives from that point on would be divided into life "before kidney failure," and "life after kidney failure." That was our new reality.

The doctor had wanted to send Bill via ambulance straight to the hospital in Athens, but Bill refused. He told the doctor that he would HAVE to come and tell me in person. He would not have it any other way. He left my classroom to go home and get a few things together. I don't remember whether I left right away or finished the day before heading to the hospital. So much of what happened that day is a blur to me now.

Bill was hospitalized at St. Mary's Hospital in Athens. He was taken to surgery where a bovine graft was placed in his left upper arm, and he was placed on hemodialysis. A nurse educated us on what it meant to have kidney failure. All of Bill's medical documents were stamped ESRD which meant End-Stage Renal Disease. END STAGE! We were shown a slideshow about living with kidney disease. The slideshow had a picture of a casket on one of the slides — warning us about the result of not eating or drinking properly while on dialysis. At that point, I lost it. I ran into the bathroom in Bill's hospital room, held my fist to my mouth, and sobbed silently. I was in a terrible nightmare; this could not be happening to Bill!

We had only been married for eight years; we were twenty-seven years old! My husband was being given a type of death sentence, and mere words cannot describe the despair we both felt. The medical professionals were educating us as much as they could on life with dialysis, and our lives changed drastically at that point. Nothing was as it had been, nor would it ever be again. Hemodialysis would require that Bill be hooked up to a machine while his blood ran through the artificial kidney. Since he was no longer able to rid his body of excess fluids and toxins, the machine would pull them directly from his blood.

Bill would go to a dialysis clinic three times a week. He was hooked up to the machine for four hours. The day of dialysis was pretty hard on him. He would often get terrible muscle cramps in the large muscles of his legs or even his stomach as several liters (sometimes 4 or more) of fluid would be removed. He had to be very careful not to take in too much fluid between sessions. I remember putting out juice cups for our water at meals. I would go back and forth into the kitchen to gulp more because I didn't want to drink extra water in front of him. Anything that melted in his mouth (including Jello) was considered a liquid. It was so difficult for a man who loved drinking large glasses of water or iced tea with his meals. He would be very weak when he returned from his treatment. By the end of the second day, he would be feeling pretty good, but then it was time for the next treatment on the third day! It became an exhausting routine week after week after week.

After several months of going to the dialysis clinic three times a week, Bill was getting depressed. He would make friends with the other patients, and occasionally, one would die. Most of them were older than Bill, and he just felt the atmosphere of the clinic was bringing him down.

Elberton Reception

The doctors offered us an opportunity for me to train so that we could bring a dialysis machine to the parsonage and do treatments at home. I was scared to death, but I hoped that Bill might improve, so I did the training during the summer months of 1982. The ladies of the church threw a surprise appreciation party for Bill in July of 1982 to try and encourage him. He had lost quite a bit of weight, but he still looked fairly strong at that point. We took one of the spare bedrooms in the parsonage and placed the large dialysis machine in there. We would roll it out into the living room for the actual treatments. Bill could watch television while he was dialyzed. A truckload of supplies would come regularly so that we kept the room stocked with artificial kidneys, syringes, tubing, saline solutions, cleaning solutions, and medicines that were needed. We had a special recliner for Bill to sit in for the treatments, and we splurged and bought a console color television — our first! Anything to distract him from the dialysis treatment was a blessing.

We decided to do dialysis every other day rather than three times a week. That would give Bill four dialysis treatments. We hoped it would help him feel a bit better. On treatment days, Bill would get things set up before I got out of school. He would even put the tubes in his own arm; the needles were as large as the end of a ball-point pen. I told you the man had courage; he never ceased to surprise me! My principal would let me leave with the students on dialysis days. I would walk into the house, wash my hands, and get the treatment started. Several times during the treatment I had to check everything, take Bill's vital signs, and record everything. Instead of dialyzing for four hours, we tried to go five. We could go slower which was easier on Bill's system. If I got the treatment started by 4:00, we would finish up between 8:00 or 9:00. Then we had to unhook Bill, clean everything, and put it all away. Bill would be pretty washed out by then, and I would be exhausted. During the treatment, I would grade papers and try to get ready for the next work day. I also fixed supper for us. Bill could eat while he was getting a treatment if he felt like it.

There are **NOT** many funny stories to tell you from that season of our lives, but I do have one. Bill needed a shot once a week, and it may have been an iron shot, but I can't remember exactly. They trained me to administer the shot into his …well…it wasn't in his arm! I practiced giving shots to an orange for a while before attempting to give him the actual shot. I hated to do it, and I was always very careful and sensitive EXCEPT for one occasion!

Anyone who has been a caregiver knows that people who do not feel well are not always nice. Bill tried his best to be positive, but even he struggled at times. He seemed to be having a hard day, and his attitude toward me had not been his best. It seemed that I could not do anything right on the treatment. I could not fix supper fast enough or bring it to him fast enough. NOTHING I did was right that day — in his perspective — and he made SURE that I knew it! Let's just say that he was not an easy patient that day.

Well, it was the night for his scheduled injection. He stood up, dropped his pants, and instead of using my normal "Nice Nurse" voice, I said,

"BEND OVER NOW!"

He looked back over his shoulder and saw me holding the syringe with an angry look on my face.

"No way, Woman! You're not touching me with that needle right now!"

He pulled his pants up, and we had a pretty decent "discussion" for a while. Eventually he apologized, and I cooled down so that I was able to "tenderly" give him the shot. We didn't laugh about it that night, but we did chuckle about it later on.

Dialyzing at home wasn't easy; it was exhausting, and it could be scary. One night I was in the kitchen finishing up our supper when all of the alarms started ringing on the dialysis machine. I ran out of the kitchen to a scene from a horror movie. One of the tubes had popped off the machine! It was dancing around like a fire hose, and Bill's blood was spraying all over the living room! Blood was on Bill; I will never forget the fear on his face! Blood was on the chair, the floor, the walls of the living room; scary just does not describe it.

"Grab the hose! Just grab it!" he yelled.

I did not wash my hands or grab my gloves. We knew he could lose too much blood very quickly and pass out. I couldn't stop to think; I just had to act.

I caught the end of the hose and stuck it back in place. Thankfully, it held. After a few seconds, the alarms stopped blaring! I checked Bill's vitals, and we began to take him off the machine. We simply couldn't risk the same thing happening again during that treatment. I scrubbed and scrubbed, and I was able to get the blood cleaned off of everything pretty well because it was fresh and had not dried. I used a lot of bleach that night. The whole house smelled like bleach for a day or two. We used bleach to regularly clean some of the equipment, so I had plenty. It goes without saying that we were both nervous wrecks after that. If we had gotten comfortable with any of this, we were NEVER comfortable again. We had seen what could happen, so we knew we had to always be on our guard.

Neither Bill nor I had ever had any true medical training before this. The summer training sessions taught us many things, but didn't really prepare us for the scenario I just described. So many things could have gone tragically wrong, but God was with us. Bill hoped that avoiding the atmosphere at the clinic would improve his mood, and it probably did help. I felt the stress of it more, but I was willing to do whatever I could to help him. Unfortunately, the many complications related to kidney failure and dialysis treatments took their toll on both of us.

Chapter Fifteen

In Sickness and In Health

***"Not only so, but we also glory in our sufferings, because we know that suffering produces perseverance; [4] perseverance, character; and character, hope."* Romans 5:3-4 NIV**

Suffering in this life may make us stronger, but it is STILL suffering!

Bill was on dialysis from early January 1982 until mid-May 1983, almost a year and a half. This may have been the most difficult and trying period of our lives, and it won't be easy for me to re-tell it. Our closest friends will remember many of these events, but most do not know the whole story. I have promised you to be honest, and I'll continue to do that, but it will mean exposing my own weakness and my own failure. That is never easy for any of us. The closer I got to this part of our story, the more dread I felt, but it must be told. I'll say it again; you cannot appreciate the miracle without knowledge of the suffering.

Hemodialysis is difficult for everyone, but some people handle it better than others. For some reason, Bill did not handle it well. He managed it the best he could, but he just continued to decline — little by little — each week. My once tall and strong husband just got weaker and weaker. I learned to walk a little slower when we went somewhere; if I didn't, he couldn't keep up. I began to help him get up out of the recliner after a treatment because he was too weak to stand on his own. His list of medications continued to grow; I still had no idea then how large it would eventually become. Those medications were also quite expensive. Bill's medical expenses became our largest expenditure and would remain that way for the rest of his life. One of his medications alone was just over $1000 per month. I look back and wonder how we survived it; I know that God saw us through. Early in our marriage Bill had his own health insurance with the conference, but that insurance was dropped at one point. For most of our marriage, the only insurance he had was mine. Bill's budgeting skills were always at work because the medical bills never stopped coming; they just got larger and larger. From the time we were twenty-seven years old, everything in our lives revolved around doctors, hospitals, medications, and medical bills. It simply became part of the fabric of our lives and our daily routines.

Bill lost weight, and his skin color changed. His hair became dry and brittle. His beautiful eyes lost their spark. We didn't take as many pictures during this period for obvious reasons. He didn't smile or laugh as much. That was one of the things that hurt me the most. I loved Bill's personality as much as anything about him; he was incredibly funny! He could make me laugh so easily, and I loved to hear him laugh. The man had an unforgettable giggle! Most of us don't laugh when we feel bad, so it should not have come as a surprise that his laughter faded when he was sick. I grieved that loss deeply.

His skin was so dry. I bought all sorts of different creams and would rub them into his arms, his legs, and his back to try and give him some relief. Many of these symptoms were side effects of his medications or the lack of hydration from limiting fluid intake. We began what I termed the "Medicine Dance." A new medicine would have a side effect, so we would treat the side effect with another medication. One med would be decreased while another one was increased. Over and over and over again, meds would be changed, and side effects would come and go. It never ended. It NEVER ended.

Several months into his dialysis treatments, Bill began to have difficulty sleeping. He would sit up in his recliner and watch television until very late before coming to bed. I had to get used to going to bed alone, something I had not done since we had gotten married. Eventually, he stopped coming to bed at all. He just sat in the recliner all night and dosed off whenever he could.

We were twenty-seven years old. My once strong and passionate husband was sitting in a recliner all night long while I lay alone in our bed. I was still healthy, and I often cried myself to sleep at night, distraught over what we had lost. These are very personal memories, but it is easy for people to avoid the realities of life with someone who is chronically ill. The truth is that I was longing for intimacy, but it was an impossibility for us at that stage, and I was still a young woman.

I would lie in bed at night and try to imagine the possible scenarios I was facing. The truth was that Bill was slowly dying in front of me; we both knew that he would not live much longer on dialysis, and we were afraid of a transplant operation. We didn't know anyone who'd had a transplant, and we were not yet ready to attempt that extreme measure. We were living in a parsonage, so I knew if Bill died, I would have to move out of the house quickly. The church would need the house for the new pastor. My teaching position was in Georgia, but all of my family was in Virginia. I had been married for eight years, and I did not want to have to go back to Virginia, but that seemed my only option.

I would plan Bill's funeral; I know that seems macabre, but that's what I did. I felt that I needed to be ready for what might happen. I was terrified. Bill had almost zero life insurance at that time — just a $1000 policy that his parents had purchased when he'd been born. We owned a car and a few pieces of furniture— nothing else. It scared him too! He told me on more than one occasion that IF he survived, we were going to buy our own house! He did not want to die and leave me with nothing, and we both knew that was becoming a very real possibility! He began to see parsonages, manses, and pastoriums as hindrances rather than benefits for pastoral families. During his later years, when he served in denominational leadership, he ALWAYS encouraged churches to give pastors a housing allowance instead. Now you know the WHY behind that.

During those lonely nights, my desire for intimacy became a huge struggle. It wasn't fair! I had married a tall and strong young man who delighted in loving me. Now, I was sleeping alone and having to walk slower so that he could keep up, and I resented it. I was angry. I was also racked with guilt. How could I be so SELFISH when the man I dearly loved was fighting for his very life! My emotions raged within me. I wanted my husband, the love of my life, to make love to me. I longed for him to take me in his arms and kiss me passionately. I wanted to get pregnant with his child. I wanted us to have a family like our friends! I wanted us to take OUR babies on picnics, to little league ballgames, to school pageants! I wanted us to grow old together. I wanted a NORMAL life!

It shames me to admit it, but at one point, on one lonely and bitter night, my thoughts took another turn into a darker place. I had cried and cried until I had no more tears.

> ***"Just go home now."***

At first it was just a ***LITTLE*** thought.

> ***"Call your daddy. He'll come and get you."***

The more I thought about it, the better it sounded. This was more than I had bargained for. Bill had changed; he was no longer the man I had married! Who could blame me? I was still young; I had needs that were not being met.

I realize now that the enemy of my soul was attacking ME at my most vulnerable place. He was the one encouraging me to RUN away from my unfortunate circumstances. Remember that none of us is immune from a spiritual attack! Keep up your guard, and always be prepared.

I entertained those thoughts for quite a while before ***GOD*** quietly reminded me of a few things.

> ***You vowed to love him IN SICKNESS AND IN HEALTH. I put the two of you together; you did NOT choose each other. I chose HIM for you, and I chose YOU for him. If you walk away from him, you are walking away from MY will for your life.***

No, I did not hear an audible voice, but I knew God was speaking into my spirit. I had no doubt, and I knew He was speaking truth.

Our circumstances did not change that night, but I no longer thought about leaving Bill. That was no longer on the table. I did begin to struggle with anger towards God. I blamed Him for putting us in this situation. I didn't believe that the sickness came from God, but I knew that my all-powerful God could certainly create a new kidney for Bill or heal the one he had! I thought I was hiding my pain and anger, but Bill knew something was wrong. He started asking me if I was okay.

"I'm FINE."

I think EVERY husband on the planet KNOWS that when his wife says, she is "FINE," she is anything BUT fine! Bill was well aware that we were not in Kansas anymore, and I was not fine!

One Saturday night after a long dialysis treatment, Bill made me sit down and talk to him. He would not allow me to run from my anger. He told me that IF he died, he needed to know that I was not angry with God. He wanted to be sure that I would continue to faithfully serve God. He said things to me that I didn't want to hear.

> ***"Karen, you've not been serving the true God; you have been serving a Sugar Daddy in the sky! You are angry with Him because you think He owes you something. You've been a 'good girl.' You have said your prayers, gone to church, and paid your tithe. He should answer your prayers and make me well! The reality is that I might die. God's plans are bigger than ours. You can't serve God because of what He DOES for you; you must serve Him simply because He is God, and you are NOT."***

He talked to me, pleaded with me, and prayed with me for HOURS — well into Sunday morning. I know that he was exhausted from his dialysis treatment, but he would not let me go. I am thankful for a husband who was willing to speak truth into my life and see me through a very dark night of soul searching. By the time we went to the Sunday morning service, I was at peace with God. I learned that God's love for me was bigger than my anger. There have been other times in my life when I questioned God's actions on my behalf, but I knew that all I had to do was confess — honestly — what I was feeling, and the healing would begin. My circumstances might not change, but my heart would be right with God.

I look back now at my younger self, and I am sympathetic to that young woman. She was in an extremely heartbreaking situation. She had never encountered anything of that magnitude, and her heart was breaking. Her beloved husband who was her safe place could no longer fill that spot. The man who had loved her so passionately could no longer give her the intimacy she was desperately craving, and she ached for what was missing in their relationship. She was looking into a dark and lonely future, and she did not know what to do. She was scared to death and felt very much alone. I wish I could go back and assure her that God was still in control, that He loved her, that He saw every tear. He understood her desires because He created her to have those desires. She was just being human. Thank God that He understands our humanity.

God was doing a work in me during those hard and lonely months, but that did not change the fact that my husband was dying right in front of me. He was weaker all the time. He continued to pastor the church, and they continued to love him for which I will always be grateful. Sometimes he would preach sitting down because he no longer had the strength to stand for extended periods. He could not visit and do all of the things he had done before, but they prayed for him and supported him which was a huge blessing to us.

By the time we were ringing in 1983, Bill and I both knew that a decision had to be made. His doctors were telling us that without a kidney transplant, Bill probably wouldn't live very long. They encouraged us to start the process and to try and find a living donor. The cadaver transplant list is very long, and a living transplant is preferred. We had great reservations about it, but we had run out of options. The longer we waited, the weaker Bill would become which would only increase the risk of the surgery.

It was time to take the risk.

Chapter Sixteen

Transplant

We began to search for a living donor in earnest. Neither I nor any of my immediate family were eligible because we had a different blood type. Bill had four older siblings, and they were all tested.

Evelyn's Convertible

Bill had always felt especially close to his youngest sister, Evelyn. I heard the story about how she had carried him on her hip as a young girl; he was "her" baby. Evelyn was ten years older than Bill. During the summer of 1973, Bill borrowed Evelyn's convertible to come and see me in Virginia while Jezebel was being repaired and refurbished. He proposed to me in that convertible! I knew that Evelyn was protective of him when on one occasion — early in our marriage — Bill and I had a slight disagreement about something when Evelyn and Burnie (her husband) were visiting us. Evelyn jumped into the conversation with a stern reminder that I needed to remember "my" place! It's funny now, but — at the time — I was a bit miffed at her comment. She was simply being the protective older sister; that's all it was.

Bill and Evelyn

Evelyn was convinced that she was going to be the one to donate a kidney! When the tests came back, she was not the best candidate and was upset about it. Within a day or two, the clinic called to announce they had mixed up the results, and Evelyn WAS the best candidate. She was thrilled! We were told that the match could not have been more perfect if they had been twins! With a ten-year age difference, we saw that as a miracle, and we thanked God for it.

Preparation for a kidney transplant takes time and lots of tests. LOTS of tests! Everything has to be right. Doctors explained to us that Bill was just getting weaker. They would have Bill and Evelyn in adjoining surgical suites, and they would open Bill first and get him ready to receive the kidney. They were not sure that he would survive the initial cutting, and they did not want to open Evelyn if Bill had died. That is the situation we were in.

In May of 1983 my parents were still working. My mama and my sister came later, but they could not get there in time for the actual surgery. Bill's siblings were all still working jobs and had children at home. Bill was the pastor of the church; we didn't have another pastor to come and be with us. There were visitors who came later, but they were not with me when Bill was taken into surgery on May 11. Burnie was in Augusta with Evelyn, but I was alone. I walked beside the hospital gurney as they wheeled him down the hallway. When I had to say goodbye, I kissed him, and I told him I was praying. I tried to smile and be encouraging, but I was so afraid. When the doors closed behind him, I turned and walked through a long corridor to the waiting room. I just broke and wept. I had been warned that he might not survive; this was serious. I don't think that I have ever felt more frightened than I did at that moment.

The surgery was a success; Bill survived, and Evelyn was fine. Praise God! One of the physicians spoke to me privately after Bill had been taken to the Intensive Care Unit to begin recovery. Earlier, I had been told that when Bill was in surgery, they were going to get a good look at the kidney they had never been able to see. They had no plans to remove it; they said it was better to leave it alone unless it was cancerous. The transplanted kidney would be placed in the lower abdomen. They simply wanted to evaluate the kidney that had failed.

> He leaned in to me and said, ***"Mrs. Jones, we had a bit of a 'moment' in the surgical suite."***
>
> ***"What do you mean?"*** I asked.
>
> ***"I told you that we wanted to locate and get a good look at Mr. Jones's kidney while we were in there. What we saw caused everyone to stop talking. Your husband is a big man. I understand he played football in high school. Is that correct?"***
>
> ***"Yes, he did,"*** I replied.
>
> ***"Well, what we found was what we call a 'rudimentary' kidney, a kidney that we would find in a developing fetus."***

My eyes got big, and I didn't know what to say.

> ***"Mrs. Jones, someone UPSTAIRS was looking out for your husband. There is no medical explanation for how a man his size could live to be twenty-seven years old with a kidney that size. We were all shocked; no one knew what to think of it!"***

God had indeed looked out for Bill! He explained that they weren't even doing widespread dialysis when Bill was a young boy. If his kidney had failed then, he would have died. Before he walked away, he also told me that I should still get my house in order. He said that Bill had so many potential health problems ahead of him that I would probably be a widow by the age of thirty, and I needed to be prepared. I didn't want to hear that, and I chose to focus on the positive at that point. The surgery had been successful; Bill had a new kidney, and we would hope for the best!

Bill was in a great deal of pain in ICU after surgery. I could only go in for a few minutes every few hours to see him. He was in the hospital for several days; it may have been almost two weeks, but I can't remember exactly. Evelyn was released earlier, but they kept Bill longer. He was improving each day, and we could hardly wait to get him home!

We arrived back at the parsonage in Elberton to a house that was filled with balloons and get-well messages! We were incredibly happy to be back home. We felt HOPE for the first time in a long time. Bill had several new medicines to take, and the doctors had tried to prepare us for our "new normal." One doctor told us that Bill probably would not die from kidney failure; he would die from a result of taking immuno-suppressing medications. They would greatly increase his risk of all types of infections, cancers, pneumonia, and many other types of illness. He had to take them to prevent organ rejection, so we had no other choice. Bill lived the rest of his life taking a bucket full of meds each and every day. He never complained about it, and he was faithful about his medications. He put his faith in God and pushed through.

For the first few years, the medications didn't seem to cause him too much trouble. Later on, that would change. I believe that those early years after that transplant were possibly the healthiest years of Bill's life. Oh, how I wish he could have enjoyed good health for his entire life.

He improved so quickly after we got home. They had stapled his surgical incision, and we had never seen anything like that. He had large staples down the front of his abdomen; it looked a little bit like Frankenstein! The resulting scar is why Daddy teased him about wrestling and gave Bill the "professional" name of ***Scarbelly***!

Those staples scared me, and I was so concerned that he would move the wrong way and something would pop open!

He had finally been able to come back to bed to sleep and leave that recliner alone! Thank God! I was thrilled to have him beside me again. Just hearing him breathe during the night was such a comfort! We had not been home but a few days, when we settled in to sleep, and he began to get a little frisky! I snuggled closer and was so happy to be able to enjoy a few snuggles and kisses with my husband. It became apparent pretty quickly that he had MORE in mind than just a few snuggles!

> ***"Good grief, Bill! You are STAPLED TOGETHER! What are you thinking?"***

I was absolutely terrified at the potential for DISASTER!

> ***"Hush Woman! I haven't felt this GOOD in over a year and half; now get over here and give me some LOVIN!"***

So, I did.

Thank God for **GOOD** staples!

Chapter Seventeen

Let the Good Times Roll!

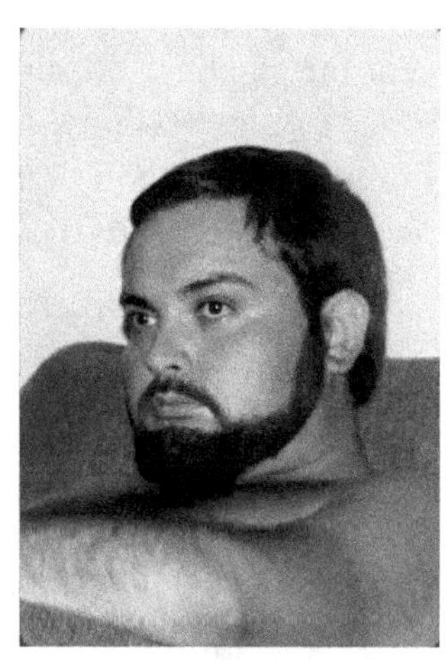

Tan Bill

It was amazing how quickly Bill gained strength and health! He was lean, and his skin color improved. His hair regained its thickness and its shine. As summer set in, he got a bit of tan as well. We took a trip to North Carolina and drove to Raleigh to visit Evelyn at her job. We were walking from the car to the office building, and the sidewalk was narrow. It was a warm summer day, and the sun was shining brightly. Bill took the lead because he knew where we were going; I just followed behind. I remember looking at him walking ahead of me. He had on a summer shirt and shorts, and he walked with strength and vitality. He looked better than I had ever seen him; he was so handsome! His hair was shiny again; his tanned arms and legs looked fit. I'd never seen him this trim and healthy. I'm telling you; he was FINE! He took my breath away! I like to think that this is what he would always have looked like had he been healthy.

When I look back through old photos, I can tell when he was doing well, and when he wasn't. Weight gain from excess fluid was never his

Healthy Bill

friend. Over the years, medications caused his cheeks to thicken and his skin to deteriorate. As he aged, his hair thinned, and the skin on his arms turned unnaturally dark. But on this beautiful summer day in Raleigh, North Carolina, my man was something to behold! He stood 6'1" tall with that massive 52" chest and 36" arms. His stomach was flat, and his legs were long and lean. My "southern" is gonna jump out here! He was PURTY, Ya'll! I was beyond proud of him. I loved him so much, and I'd come so close to losing him! My heart was filled with gratitude for the GIFT of having him alive AND so full of strength!

He had energy, and his eyes sparkled again. He was full of mischief and kept me giggling. Bill always loved to sing, and he enjoyed singing crazy songs to me. When we were dating, he would sing this silly song from Jimmy Soul, "If You Wanna Be Happy." I'd never heard it before, but it tickled him to death to sing it to me. The chorus goes like this,

"If you wanna be happy for the rest of your life

NEVER make a pretty woman your wife

So from my personal point of view

Get an ugly girl to marry you!"[1]

Now, it did NOTHING for my self-esteem for him to sing THAT to me! Seriously, I knew he was joking, and he got a kick out of my resistance to the lyrics. Bill loved to ADD his own personal touch to whatever he sang, so he often added lines to the originals. Most of his additions would not be appropriate for me to list here; he could be quite the sneaky guy! He knew that I loved it! He would sing, and I would laugh. What could be better than that!

He also made up songs of his own — all the time. He sang to me in the kitchen, in the bathroom, in the bedroom, in the car. It didn't matter.

1 1963 Jimmy Soul, written by Rafael de Leon and adapted by Joseph Royster, Carmella Guida and Frank Guida.

Most of "those" songs cannot be repeated either! What a guy! That's what kept us laughing together.

We always listened to the radio in the car, and we sang together. We had started that when we were dating. Most folks would assume that we always listened to gospel music or sacred music, but Bill LOVED Motown! We listened to all the great Motown songs, oldies from the '60s and '70s, Chicago, The Beatles, The Monkees, The Association. He also liked smooth jazz and bluegrass! We enjoyed it all.

His very favorite song to sing to me was "When a Man Loves a Woman," and he only liked the Percy Sledge version. Bill would half sing and half talk a dialogue of his own throughout the song that was hysterical! I once told him that if he died, I would be crushed to hear that song again. Thankfully, that has not been the case; I just wish I had a video of him doing it. I was always laughing too hard to record it. He did it one night when my mama was in the car, and she laughed until she cried! She loved Bill and his foolishness! We all did.

During that first year of recovery we just enjoyed LIFE together! Kidney failure, dialysis, and the transplant had changed Bill. He was more handsome than ever, and we were enjoying each other again. His passion returned, and we loved each other as never before. Having lost the ability to express our love completely made its return all the more precious. I certainly never took our intimacy for granted because we had lost it for a season, and I knew we had no guarantees. Bill was incredibly thankful to have his vitality restored, and he adored loving me. We both had JOY again! Laughter had returned to us, and we were so grateful, but Bill was different. He had stared death in the eye, and he had beaten it! He was more driven after that experience. He knew life had an expiration date, and he knew that his might come sooner rather than later.

He wanted to enjoy life MORE! On our visits back and forth to Augusta in preparation for the transplant, we would drive over a large lake. There were usually several pontoon boats on the lake.

"If I survive this, I want to buy a pontoon boat!"

He announced this while driving over the lake one day. I questioned how we could afford a boat! We had been tucking money aside for a trip to Hawaii on our tenth anniversary which was coming up in June of 1984.

He promised me that if we could use that money to buy a boat that he would take me to Hawaii later. He did keep his word on that. We celebrated our twentieth anniversary on a wonderful trip to several Hawaiian Islands. Bill planned every aspect of the trip, and it was a fantastic one!

Bill on Pontoon Boat

Bill never learned how to swim. He grew up near the ocean and adored being on the water, but he absolutely could not swim! I tried on numerous occasions to teach him, but the man sank like a rock no matter what we tried! I've never known anyone with less buoyancy! He didn't want a fast boat; he wanted a large pontoon where we could take family and friends out on the lake, and where he could fish while I relaxed on one of the couches and read a book or took a nap.

We bought that boat, and we enjoyed it tremendously for many years! We used it on church outings as well. Bill laughed and said he should name the boat, "Visitation." Then he could tell the congregation that he had been out on "Visitation" all weekend! Don't get upset; he never did that, but we laughed about the possibility of it!

Karen on Pontoon Boat

The boat provided an opportunity for the two of us to get away from the stresses of life. We would hitch the boat to Bill's truck, pack a couple of sandwiches and drinks in the cooler and take off! We did a lot of lovin' on that boat too, and we would come back to our home sun-warmed and totally fulfilled and happy.

Everything was absolutely wonderful, until it wasn't.

Chapter Eighteen

Storms Roll In

After Bill had adjusted to this new life he had been given, he began to talk about us pursuing pregnancy again. About two years had passed since his kidney failure. We were nearly thirty years old, and the clock was ticking. Our doctor wanted to run new tests on Bill. I still remember seeing tears in the eyes of the nurse as she followed the doctor back into the room where we'd been waiting. She glanced at me and quickly averted her eyes. I KNEW before the doctor said one word.

No sperm. There were NO sperm; nothing. The kidney failure, and the anti-rejection meds had taken care of whatever sperm he'd had before. The doctor looked at us and said very clearly, "It will be impossible for you to have biological children."

Bill was broken, and I was in tears when the doctor left the room. The nurse hugged me, and said, "God still does miracles!"

We believed in miracles, and we needed one. The desire to have a child was so strong in both of us. Most of our friends had children in elementary school at this time. My younger sister had already had a child. It wouldn't be long before my "baby" brother married and had a child. We kept praying, and we kept trying. The hope for a miracle remained alive for Bill much longer than it did for me, but I will share more about that later.

Bill in Elberton

Bill was as alive as he had ever been. He had more strength and energy than I had ever seen before. He was on fire for God and filled with drive and passion. That passion drew new people to church, and it fueled more revival fires! God's Spirit was moving, and change was in the air!

It's what every pastor longs for, but it can bring division in the church. We absolutely loved the church where we were planted, and they had loved on us and cared for us during Bill's illness. We made dear friends who are still precious to us today. Souls were saved, and lives were changed. The blessings of those years cannot and will not be denied, but problems did arise.

With the increase in Bill's drive and passion, came less of a willingness to "play" church or placate church members. He was less apt to wait for folks to come around to a new way of doing things. His heart was always in the right place, and He was pushing the congregation into deeper worship and openness to the moving of God's Spirit. He was also challenging some of the cultural "norms" of the day which was met with resistance by some. Bill longed for a church filled with young and old, black and white, rich and poor.

"There are NO throwaway people!"

I cannot tell you how many times I heard Bill say that! He felt it to his innermost core.

Bill had a heart for everyone! He reached out to those who were rejected by others and saw people the way Jesus saw them. Their financial status or the color of their skin did not matter to him.

Most of the congregation was on fire and on the move, but there were many who did not agree with either Bill's methods or his timing. The point is that we came to a roadblock that could not be moved. Bill's preaching was true, and He was doing his very best to follow God's leading. He had a vision for the direction of this congregation, but everyone did not share his vision. Tension mounted, and things became increasingly contentious.

After several painful and extremely stressful months, we knew that something had to give. We were offered a church in the Atlanta area, and we even had a couple from our church staff who were willing to move with us and help us in that church. We drove to Atlanta, looked at the church and the parsonage, and met with church leadership. They wanted us to come and offered us an acceptable salary package. It looked good! After the visit, we tried everything we could to get peace about moving, but God would not give it to us. He had not released us from Elberton, and our hearts were heavy.

During that very difficult season, God sent many wonderful people to lift us up and encourage us. The letters, the phone calls, and the visits from loving church members, pastors from other denominations, and friends from across the country held up our weary arms when our strength was gone. They prayed for us; they stood by us, and they kept us going when we wanted to give up. I recently found this letter from a dear college friend and his wife, Rev. Gary Osteen and Audrie. It is dated October 15, 1984, and it was in a box of Bill's belongings. He had kept it for over forty years!

> ***I have been thinking about you much lately. I want you to know that I am praying for you. I know you are going thru a tough time, and the enemy is attacking you on every side. Many times in an attack, all we can do is to stand firm. "Having done all, stand."***
>
> ***All you can do is your best and leave the rest up to God. Every confrontation is to make us stronger and more like Christ. I want to encourage you to guard against bitterness. It can raise its ugly head and defile many. God is with you, and He has not left you.***
>
> ***If I can ever help you in any other way than praying, just let me know. I believe in you and the calling and ministry that you have. I believe in your wife, and she is to be commended for her standing by you during confrontation. I believe God has some great things planned for you. I believe it is getting better. One way or another, it will be better. We love you and you are special to us.***

One Saturday night, our conference superintendent came by the parsonage. He sat down and spoke openly to us.

> ***"Bill, I have spent the afternoon visiting with many of the church board members. They are not going to relent in their opposition. I know you have a large portion of the congregation behind you, so I recommend that you start a second church in Elberton. You will have the full backing of the conference board, and we will help financially if we can. I am willing to come tomorrow and announce this in the church service. I believe if you stay here, you are only going to bring more stress on you and Karen. This town is big enough to support two of our churches. Why don't you start fresh with those who share your vision and build a new church?"***

Neither of us had ever wanted to be a part of a church split; it's not who we were. Bill would hear of a church split somewhere, and it always saddened him. We heard what he was saying, but we didn't WANT to hear it. Remember that Bill always believed in operating under authority. Here was the man in authority coming and expressing his belief with the full support of the conference board behind him. He was supportive of us and encouraged us to go after the vision with all we had. It was a huge blessing to have his love and support. Bill felt that he needed to continue to operate under the authority of our conference leadership; they had stood beside us through all of this. We had tried to move away from Elberton, but that door had closed because we could not get peace. God had given us a powerful vision for the area, and we simply could not abandon it.

That Sunday morning service was one of the most difficult services I have ever attended. You could hear a pin drop after the superintendent made the announcement. The congregation was told that Bill and I would be starting a new church the very next Sunday — the location would be announced at some point in the upcoming week. Anyone was welcome to join the new church — yet to be named. The conference board supported this decision and blessed the new church plant. After the service, I just went to the front of the church and stood near Bill; we did not go to the vestibule to shake hands as we had always done. Many folks came up to us with tears in their eyes and said they would be with us the next Sunday. That was encouraging because we were about to jump into waters we had never navigated before!

Bill was adamant that we would not take anything from the existing church. Bill set it up so that we could have our initial service at the 4-H center in Elberton. We started with absolutely nothing except God's blessing. What else did we need? It was truly miraculous to see how God moved through individuals and local businesses to supply needs along the way. There were so many things that we had taken for granted — a pulpit, chairs, songbooks, microphones, a piano! Our faith grew as we watched God provide over and over again for our new congregation.

Closing Thoughts:

We moved around like the Israelites for several years before we were able to purchase a beautiful piece of property on the edge of town. We presently have a large multi-purpose building which houses the sanctuary, a fellowship hall, church offices, and classrooms as well. We also have cabins for temporary shelter ministry at the back of the property. Bill had wonderful plans for multiple buildings on the property, and I hope that those dreams will someday come to pass.

Today there are two solid congregations in Elberton. Two churches filled with people who love God and are doing their best to serve Him and reach a town, a county, and northeast Georgia for Christ.

People are not perfect. Pastors are not perfect, and congregations are not perfect. Many times, personality conflicts can surface and get in the way of the move of God. Wherever we were, Bill always loved his congregants like family. He was dedicated to teaching and preaching the truth and stretching them as much as possible. He was also not afraid to correct them when needed, and he never, ever ran from a conflict. Our earthly fathers often have to bring correction; our Heavenly Father does as well. A true pastor will need to bring correction — and sometimes discipline — to his church members. That is what Jesus would do. Jesus showed love and grace to the woman caught in adultery, but we cannot forget that He also told her to "go and sin no more."

A dear friend sent me a text not long ago, and this was her description of Bill.

> ***"His life affected so many for the Kingdom of God. His was a theology of 'all in.' Brother Bill challenged everyone to step up to a higher level of service and surrender."***

Bill would have been the one to run into a burning building for someone. I'm not sure I can say that about myself. I can back off at times to avoid an issue, but not my "warrior" husband. Many years later when he was handling a very contentious conference issue, I asked him if he could just ease up a little bit to bring less stress on himself. He looked me straight in the eye, and without any hesitation whatsoever, he responded.

> ***"That's not who I am. It's not who God has called me to be. Sometimes things need to be dealt with. It's not easy, and I don't enjoy it, but I cannot run from it. I just can't."***

Bill was only twenty-three years old when we moved to Elberton. He was very young to have that pastoral assignment, but he gave it his very best. He loved the church, and he worked hard to be a good pastor to them. When he saw areas that he felt could be improved or areas where growth was needed, he faced them head-on and without hesitation. Perhaps he could have moved a bit slower when changes needed to be made; that is certainly a possibility. Did correction need to come in a few instances? Absolutely, I have no doubt about that. More than forty years have passed since that sad time, so it does no good to dwell on it. Some apologies have come our way over the years, and we have responded in kind. I am not minimizing the attack against Bill; some things were said about him that simply were not true. That was wrong, and it hurt his reputation for years.

In recent years, I have tried my best to focus on the good things that happened to us in our early years of Elberton and try to forget the painful things that were said and done. That congregation loved us and ministered to us through Bill's first kidney failure; they prayed diligently for us to have a child. Those kindnesses have never been forgotten. I know that Bill and I both learned lessons from that stressful time in ministry. Bill served in conference leadership for many years, and I cannot tell you the times that he ministered to churches mired in conflict, and he ministered to the congregations and to the pastors from ***experience***. He knew where they were; he knew what they were going through, and he could lead with strength gained from his own trials.

God can take WHATEVER we face — no matter how painful it might be -and use it for good.

Chapter Nineteen

Singing Baby Blues

The Lighthouse Organization Service

We organized The Lighthouse on December 2, 1984, with more than thirty households represented. It was a whirlwind of activity to find locations for services, to organize church members to set up and take down equipment for every single service! We had a solid group of the most dedicated folks anyone could ever wish for. Bill and I were both so thankful for several faithful senior saints who shared our vision! Some had been charter members of the other church and would now become charter members of the new church. They stepped out of their comfort zone to follow the vision. Praise God! Without the love and faithfulness of both the young and the old, Bill and I could never have built the new church; it was truly a congregational effort.

It was a joy to have so many church members catch the vision and faithfully run the race with us! What freedom we experienced in that! The church has seen many changes over the past four decades, but one thing has remained and that is a faithful congregation who values and respects pastoral leadership. If Bill planted anything in them, I know he did

THAT! Whenever I see the church bless the current pastor — who grew up under Bill's ministry — my heart overflows with JOY!

Our first home

Bill was extremely busy during those early years at The Lighthouse, but he was totally fulfilled in that ministry. We did buy the house he had always promised me! It was a little brick ranch house that had been repossessed and needed a lot of work. That is the only way we could afford to purchase it! Bill was starting a new church without a guaranteed salary, and I was a school teacher. We were not the BEST credit risks at the time! Church members pitched in to help us clean up that little house which made the work more like fun! How wonderful it was to paint a room or change a rug without having to go through a committee to get permission first! We were making a house a home — OUR home. I loved it, and I knew that Bill was taking every step he could to give me a measure of security if he died first. That thought was always in the back of our minds; it was hard to get away from it. Even so, we were enjoying every moment of building our new church and settling into the first home of our very own.

The only thing lacking from our happiness was a child. My womb and our arms were still empty; the longing to be parents was never far from our hearts.

We were just a small congregation, but we had many talented singers and actors, and we were always looking for new songs, worship dances, skits, or plays to produce. We serve a creative God, and it was our desire to incorporate the arts into our worship as much as possible. Our biggest creative endeavor was a musical called "The Bride" which was an allegorical tale about the bride of Christ and Satan's attacks against the Church. It was written by Dony and Reba Rambo McGuire who lived and ministered in Atlanta at the time. We were all familiar with the significant musical impact of Dottie Rambo, Reba's mom, on gospel music. We loved doing that musical, and we even took it on the road to several different churches. The songs and the message were incredibly powerful.

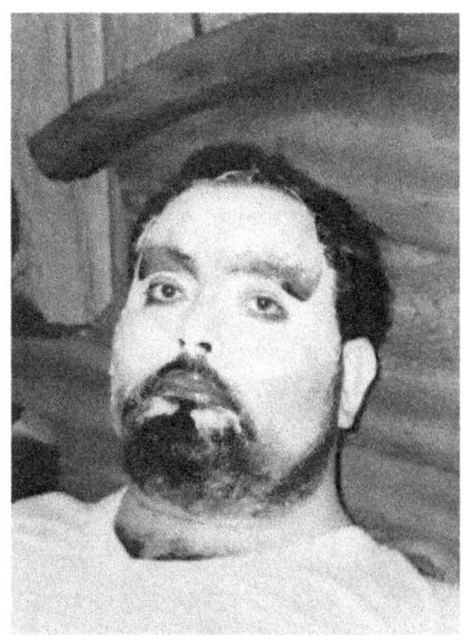

Bill's Devil Make-up

By the way, I played the "Bride of Christ" and guess who played the devil? Yes! None other than the church pastor, my own Bill! Have mercy, he played a scary devil! After my daddy saw the play, he said it would be a week or two before he could even LIKE Bill again! LOL!

Sometime in the early 1990's, we had an opportunity to schedule Dony and Reba for a concert at our church. Since many in the community had come to see "The Bride" production, we knew they would come to see Dony and Reba in person. We were thrilled to welcome them; they were Grammy award winners! Our church building was newly built, and Reba was struggling with paint fumes affecting her voice that night. I did not have a chance to meet Reba before the service, but I planned to introduce myself at the close. God had other plans.

At some point during the service, Reba stopped singing and began to minister to the congregation. She stopped and made eye contact with me. She asked me to come to the front of the church where she began to pray for me — not knowing who I was or anything about me.

Suddenly, she stopped praying.

> She looked at me and said, ***"I see a baby falling out of a sheet into your arms."***

At that point, most of the congregation who knew our struggle with infertility began to shout! I mean, we were Pentecostals, so shouting was nothing new! THIS was like REVIVAL! WhooHOO!

The only problem is that I was NOT shouting! I was actually angry about it. I was tired of infertility. I was tired of going up for prayer. I was tired of prophesies that weren't coming true. I was in my mid-thirties without a child; the dream was beginning to die inside of me. We had even begun to look into private adoption as well. With Bill's health issues, we could not go through an agency. We had faced ***NOTHING*** but disappointment from every avenue.

Reba said those words with conviction, but I was not convinced. The shouts behind me did not sway me. My heart had become hardened, and it got worse before it got better.

Approximately ***five years*** would pass before I would speak to Reba again. During those five years, we had several failed adoption attempts. Two of them nearly broke me. Our lawyer contacted us about a young girl who had recently discovered she was pregnant. She wanted to give up the baby, and our lawyer asked us to consider it. We were excited about this possibility and agreed with very little hesitation! This would be an infant we could adopt at birth! That is huge! We had already learned that the easy availability of abortions in the United States had greatly decreased the possibility of adopting a newborn.

A few weeks passed before I heard from the lawyer again. He called me one day when Bill was away. He was crying when he told me that the girl's family physician had encouraged her to have an abortion. He thought she was too young to carry a baby and to have to deal with "all of that." Her parents respected his opinion, and the abortion was scheduled for the next morning.

When I hung up the phone, I fell to the floor and completely lost it. I truly believe I had a breakdown. I wasn't just crying; I was screaming and crying! I was afraid the neighbors would hear and call the police! I cried out to God and pleaded for the life of that unborn child! I even tried to make deals with God!

> ***"Save the baby, and let the mother keep it! Just don't let that baby die tomorrow!"***

The truth is that God was crying with me. This girl was planning to exercise her own free will, and she was following the advice of a doctor she trusted. We often make huge mistakes in life which break the heart of God, but He does not always intervene in our decisions. These are the things that we do not understand this side of Heaven.

I went to school the next day. I knew the time for the scheduled abortion. I looked at my students in the classroom and in the hallways, knowing that the baby I LONGED to love and to care for, the baby I already had envisioned in our home, the baby that Bill wanted to dedicate to the Lord and raise to serve Jesus was being slaughtered in a doctor's office. It was nearly impossible for me to hold in my tears; my heart was breaking inside of me! That baby's innocent blood was being shed unnecessarily to make a young girl's life more convenient. I am not angry at the girl; she was a teen-ager. I am angry at the doctor who convinced her to make this terrible mistake! I know that I will meet that baby in Heaven some day; I believe that God meant for us to have that child. I never carried him or her in my womb, but I had carried that baby in my heart, even if it was for only a few weeks.

There were a couple of times we heard about possible adoption opportunities that fizzled out before we could actually make a decision. There was one more adoption attempt that seemed to be a sure thing; we even met with the birthmother. She was older, and her husband was in jail. She had gotten pregnant and felt that she could not keep this child due to the circumstances. She looked at both of us and assured us that she would not back out. Things were moving right along, and we were getting more and more excited as we approached the expected birth date.

Once again, a phone call changed everything. The birth mom called me and said that she had been out somewhere and had gotten on an elevator with another woman. Naturally, a discussion began about the pregnancy. When the woman on the elevator found out that the birth mom was planning to give away the child, she condemned her for that decision and made her feel guilty!

> ***"I'm not saying that I am going to back out, but that woman made me feel really terrible! I'm not sure if I'm doing the right thing; I need to think about it and wanted to talk to you."***

When I hung up the phone, I knew it was over. I don't remember a breakdown like I had with the abortion situation, but my heart hardened a bit more. When Bill got home, I told him I was through with adoption! I actually told him that God would have to ***drop*** a baby on our porch in a basket with a ***BOW*** before I would reconsider! Remember ***that***; just remember it!

Bill told me much later that he was contacted a time or two after that, and he told the lawyer that he just couldn't tell me. He knew my heart was too fragile to handle another disappointment. Little did we know what was on the horizon. God was about to take us on a ride that we couldn't have imagined in our wildest dreams! We would never have believed it ourselves unless we had lived it!

Buckle up, Folks! We were on the verge of seeing some mighty miracles, but one ***small*** fly in the ointment would have to be dealt with first.

Chapter Twenty

The Sound of Silence

Letter from Karen August 25, 1973

I can't sing very well, but at least I'll sing for God. …I'd love to be able to really sing — I enjoy it so much, and I get so frustrated by my inability to do it well. All I can do is try.

Something strange began to happen to me in the spring and summer of 1995. It seemed that I could not keep my throat clear. Every time I answered the phone, the person on the other end would ask if I had been asleep. It was odd. It felt like my throat was clogged up, and it was affecting my voice.

Karen Singing

I have been a singer all of my life; it is something that brings me great joy! Daddy would take me to the little local country store when I was a toddler. He would set me up on the counter, and I would sing "One-eyed, One-horned, Flying Purple People Eater"[1] to the old geezers sitting around and chewing the fat. It is one of my earliest memories. I sang in church all my life. Bill and I sang together as we dated and throughout our marriage.

1 Sheb Wooley, MGM

I am not a trained singer — other than glee club in high school. I entered talent contests and lost. I came to Emmanuel with a great desire to sing in the college choir, but I didn't pass the audition, and it crushed me. I can assure you that my self-confidence was LOW when it came to singing. After failing the college audition, I pretty much decided never to sing a solo again. Bill loved my voice, and he encouraged me to sing; a future sister-in-law also encouraged me to sing. That's why I sang to him in our wedding. I knew that he would love it whether anyone else did or not.

When we started The Lighthouse, folks began to respond to my singing differently. I began to feel that my voice was blessing them, and that is what I wanted more than anything. God helped me to overcome my fears and sing boldly for Him. Bill was always my biggest supporter. Being able to minister to others in song has always been one of the greatest joys in my life! There have been people and circumstances that have tried to shut down my singing ministry all of my adult life, and Bill stood in the gap and would not allow it!

"Sing it, Girl" he often said as I started a song.

Karen Singing Boldly

His voice would boom out in the congregation, and I would feel his love surrounding me and supporting me in that moment. I hope he knows how much it meant for me to hear that.

Before the end of that summer, I really could no longer sing. I thought I was getting sick with something, and Bill encouraged me to make an appointment. After school started it only got worse. By the time I saw the doctor, I could barely whisper. My voice would sort of "cut in and cut out." I might be mid-word and nothing would come out. My mouth would move without sound. It took a great deal of effort to get the words out, and I was getting scared.

My doctor agreed that something was very wrong, and he sent me to a specialist in Augusta. I was diagnosed with severe nodules on both vocal cords. The diagnosis was concerning. He explained what nodules were and how they were inhibiting my speech. He wanted to try speech therapy first to see if we could get them to reduce in size. He explained surgical options might be looming in the future. He also explained to me that I could lose my voice completely. He knew that I was a teacher and depended on my voice.

> ***"Mrs. Jones, I don't know if you will ever be able to sing again, and that's not my priority. My priority is to help you continue to teach and keep your career."***

You cannot imagine what that did to me. My heart was singing! My ministry was singing! Part of our love story was singing!

Bill continued to sing as we drove down the road together. I remember turning my head away and pretending to look out the window so that he would not see me cry. My heart was breaking because I could no longer sing with him. I was being silenced against my will!

I love to talk and tell stories! I have never been a quiet person! I found myself surrounded by people who were talking, and I could not contribute to the conversation. I could no longer go through a drive-thru because they could not hear me. I would write instructions on the board in the classroom because the students could not hear me. Sometimes I would motion for students to come to me; I would whisper in their ear, and they could give the instructions. I had to be careful, though, because I learned in therapy that whispering is NOT good for our vocal cords. I mainly just wrote notes.

I was teaching in the high school by then, and it was a sad day when the head of the department came to see me.

> ***"Karen, I think you are going to need to consider disability retirement. You simply can't continue to teach if you cannot talk."***

She was a dear Christian friend of mine, and her heart was breaking for me. I knew I was reaching a place where I could not go on.

I prayed and prayed during those months of silence.

> Sometimes I pleaded with God for my voice, but eventually, my prayer became, ***"Lord, I believe. Help my unbelief. Please heal me; I want my voice back! If you do not, I will find another way to praise you. The silence will NOT stop my praise!"***

Many folks said to me during this time that they KNEW I was going to be healed. I wanted to believe them, but God was not giving me any of those assurances. I could not fully have enough faith for that, but I felt God's peace when I prayed the prayer I shared above. It became a daily prayer for me, a declaration of my intent to find a new way to praise if I had to.

October arrived, and my voice was even worse. I had been faithfully going to speech therapy in Augusta for several months with a caring therapist. I will say that I learned quite a few things during those months of therapy that I still practice today. Our ability to speak and sing is a gift from God, and we do have to protect our vocal cords; they can be injured easily.

She was concerned with what was happening, and we made an appointment for me to see the doctor on the following Monday to set things in motion for vocal cord surgery. The therapy had not been effective. I was told that even with laser surgery, my cords would be scarred. My voice would be different, and there was still a possibility that it would be completely lost.

The weekend before that Monday appointment, my voice was completely gone. It never "cut in" at all. If I pushed enough air through, there was a slight scratchy whisper, but no real voice. All seemed lost.

I went to bed on Sunday night, and I prayed again.

> ***"Lord, I believe. Help my unbelief! Please heal me; restore my voice. That's my desire, but I will praise you either way; I will find a way."***

I went to sleep not having any idea what was about to happen.

On Monday morning, Bill got up first. He had to run an errand or two for the church before we drove to Augusta. I got out of bed and started getting ready. We had a little dog at the time, a Pekingese/poodle-mix named Peaches. She had gotten used to my scratchy whisper over time. She was looking up at me with a questioning expression.

"Have you got to go pee-pee?" I asked.

Wait a minute! What???

> ***"Have you got to go pee-pee?"***

I said again, but it came out as clear as a bell! No scratchiness! No whisper! No cutting in and cutting out. CLEAR! CLEAR!

I started dancing around that kitchen as Peaches looked at me like I had lost my mind!

> ***"Have you got to go pee-pee??????"***

I kept saying that ridiculous phrase over and over and laughing!

I had not heard my own CLEAR voice in almost ***nine months***!

I told you that God has a sense of humor! Every time I have shared this testimony of the fabulous miracle of my voice restoration, I have to share the wonderful FIRST words of my healing!

> ***"Have you got to go pee-pee?"***

Yes, Friends. Those were my MIRACLE words!

I called Bill and started talking to him. It actually took a few seconds before it dawned on him.

> ***"Your voice! Your voice! It's back!"***

I told him the story, and we laughed and praised together. I asked him what we were going to do about the appointment.

> ***"We're going to keep it! We are going to let the doctor confirm what God has done!"***

We drove to Augusta and went first to the doctor who had planned to schedule the surgery. It was rather humorous because he listened to me and he examined me.

> ***"Well, you have no nodules; they are COMPLETELY gone. There is one small red spot on one vocal cord. I will just give you a prescription that should clear that up in no time. Why are you here again? The appointment says "surgery," but you don't' need surgery!"***

We explained to the best of our ability what had happened. I'm not sure he believed it, but he told me that I did not have to come back and see him anymore. He thought that speech therapy had done the trick! He was **WRONG**! He told me to go back home, and to keep teaching and singing! I'd never heard words that made me so happy before.

We decided to drive over to the hospital to see my speech therapist. When I walked into the office complex, I saw her talking to someone, and her back was turned to me. I walked up behind her and said something. She had ***never*** actually heard my normal voice, so she did not recognize it. When she turned around and saw me, she was stunned! She was so amazed, she went to the head of the speech department at the hospital and brought her to meet me. This woman had been a speech therapist for twenty-five years! She looked at my records, and heard the story. She told me that it was impossible for nodules of that size to go away overnight. It was simply IMPOSSIBLE.

> ***"For with God nothing (is or ever) shall be impossible."***
> **(Luke 1:37 Amplified Bible)**

I continued to teach for twenty-three more years, and I am still singing today (thirty years later). God's miracle of restoration was COMPLETE. I have never stopped praising Him for the gift of speech and the gift of song! Oh my, I am crying as I type these words.

My JOY is singing, and losing that ability put me in a dark place for about nine long months. Um…nine months may be a significant number because God was about to give us a gift that usually takes about nine months to develop. There was definitely LIGHT at the end of my dark tunnel!

Chapter Twenty-one

Westward Bound!

It was a beautiful day in February 1996, the kind of day that gives false hope of an early spring. The sun was shining, and it was warm in northeast Georgia. I was piddling around the house, and Bill was at the church getting ready for some type of men's meeting, I think. I remember being happy as I went from task to task; it was just one of those GOOD days!

The wall phone in our kitchen rang. Normally, I did not answer the phone when Bill was gone. Most calls were for him, and I hated to talk on the phone and take messages for him. I still don't like to make phone calls and just chat. Thankfully, we had an answering machine by then, and I could let the machine catch it. For some reason, and I can only believe it was God, I walked into the kitchen and picked up the receiver. I distinctly remember thinking, "Why am I answering this phone?"

"Hello? Is this the residence of Pastor Bill Jones?"

I responded, ***"Yes, it is."***

"Well, Hello! Is this his wife?"

The voice on the other end was distinctly southern, and I struggled to recognize it.

"Yes, this is Karen."

"Karen, this is Reba Rambo McGuire! How are you doing?"

To say that I was shocked is an understatement! I could not imagine why she was calling. I began to assume that maybe they were coming this way, and she was trying to book another service. We had had absolutely no contact with them whatsoever for almost five years. FIVE YEARS!

She chatted with me casually for a few minutes. She and Dony lived in Nashville now; they were actually in an on-going revival meeting in California. I continued to wonder why in the world she had called me, then she dropped the bomb.

> ***"Karen, this church in California sponsors a home for unwed mothers. There is a young woman here who is about to deliver, and I believe God told me that this baby is yours."***

Things froze. I mean the world stopped spinning for just a moment. Something stirred in me that I had not felt for quite a while — maybe it was hope.

> ***"I know you'll think I'm crazy, but when I found out about this girl, God gave me a vision about the prophecy I gave you! I was back in your church in Georgia; I could smell the paint and the sawdust, and I remembered word for word the prophecy about a baby falling out of a sheet into your arms!"***

Okay, this WAS crazy! My mind simply could not process this.

> ***"I am sorry that I could not recall your names, so I called my secretary in Nashville. I asked her to go through our records and fax me all the names of churches/pastors we had visited in Georgia over the past several years. When I scanned through the names and saw 'Rev. Bill Jones / The Lighthouse,' I KNEW! This is your baby! Karen, this is YOUR BABY!"***

She went even further. She told me that after that vision, she went and met the birth mother herself. She started trying to explain the vision to this young woman (in her twenties), but before she could even tell the entire story, she was interrupted. The birthmother told Reba that God had already spoken to her that Dony and Reba had something to do with the adoption. You see, the birth mom had already turned down a couple of prospective couples, and the birth was imminent (or so they thought). The birth mom thought that maybe Dony and Reba were going to adopt the baby!

She told Reba that whatever Reba said, she would do. She would accept us as the adoptive parents — sight unseen!

I was speechless which doesn't happen often. What could I say to this fantastic series of events? Everything Reba had told me was just so unbelievable! I couldn't wrap my brain around all of it. I mumbled something about needing to talk to Bill. Reba said she understood, but she emphasized that the baby was due any day, and we needed to act quickly.

When Bill walked in the door, I told him that he'd better sit down. I guess he saw the look of shock on my face, and he thought someone had died! I did my best to relay the conversation, and he was as stunned as I was. I told him that this was such an incredible set of circumstances that I thought we would have to pursue it. I had no faith that we would actually get a baby; I thought maybe God wanted us to minister to the birth mother. We were forty-one years old and liked to take naps! I wasn't sure I wanted an infant at my age; I really couldn't imagine it. I had just started looking into an opportunity to earn my master's degree, and a baby didn't figure into that. I had shut my door to that possibility, but a HUGE window was being opened without my help!

Bill was shocked that I would even consider it. He began to cry on the couch. We held each other and just sat "in the moment." We prayed together for God's guidance and God's will. I am thankful for that time of quiet solitude with God because we were about to get on a rollercoaster of epic proportions! We had spent quite a bit of money on doctor bills for my recent speech therapy sessions, plus the trips each week back and forth to Augusta, and we'd had car trouble as well. Funds were low, and we had no idea how we would get to California and afford to be there for a few days. We had never had a home study done; we had no nursery ready. The obstacles were all around us, BUT GOD! But...God! All we could do was pray and keep walking, and that's what we did. We were about to witness a series of miracles unlike anything we had ever seen before, and we had already seen some GREAT ones!

The next couple of weeks were unbelievable! We called Reba the next day and said we were willing to come to California. The day after that, she called us and told us that their ministry was going to purchase the airline tickets for us! That was the first obstacle to fall; our plane fare was paid for! Hallelujah!

Bill made phone calls all day long! Remember that this was before we had cell phones! He was told that it would take six months to get the home study done and all of the legal paperwork to go to California and get a baby! Bill replied that we needed it done in a matter of DAYS! Folks thought he was CRAZY! Phone call after phone call! Faxed papers back and forth — we were not using computers yet in our house. We had to get our doctor to sign a document that declared Bill was healthy enough to be a father. Praise God for a good Christian doctor who had prayed with us for a child and who was excited to do that for us!

Elberton is a small town, and people knew us. Folks went out of their way to help us get paperwork done. The home study was completed in record time! Churches and Sunday School classes across town took up collections and gave us money to help us with the trip! The whole town was rooting for us! They were almost as excited as we were! It was amazing to just see what God was doing.

My high school principal worked with me to line up a long-term substitute. I wrote weeks of lesson plans not knowing how long I might be out. I knew we could not afford for me to take a full pregnancy leave, but I wanted to stay with the baby (***IF*** we brought one home) as long as I could. I did not qualify for a paid maternity leave since it was an adoption. Things may be different now, but that's how it was then. I still had no assurance we would actually get a baby, but I had no doubts about making this trip to California. God was doing SOMETHING; I was absolutely sure about that.

The clock was ticking; the doctor had estimated the baby's arrival, and we desperately wanted to get to California. The birthmother had said we could be at the birth if we got there in time! We had our bags packed and ready (just like parents do when they are expecting) for the moment when Bill would get the "go ahead" from the lawyers (one in Georgia and another in California) that the paperwork was complete. We didn't have enough money for ONE lawyer, much less TWO! Praise God for lawyers who gave us discounted rates and allowed us to pay them in installments!

I was in the middle of a lesson with one of my classes when they paged me to take a call in the office. I ran down the hallway to take the call. Bill told me that everything was ready, and we needed to get to the Atlanta airport to catch our flight that evening! Dony and Reba had purchased the tickets and had everything set up at the airport for us.

My students and colleagues had been walking this "walk" with me, and they were all excited for me. When I walked out of my classroom that day, students and teachers lined up to cheer me on! It was so exciting, and I am incredibly thankful that they shared my joy and excitement. I ran to my car and rushed home to meet Bill.

We were on our way! California, here we come!

The Joneses were westward bound!

Chapter Twenty-two

Baby Makes Three Part I

Letter from Karen August 25, 1973

> ***If things work out — someday you and I will share the ultimate — we'll have a baby- the product of OUR love, and we'll dedicate him to God because he'll be a gift from God.***

A miracle was on the way! We could not have been more excited as we jumped in the car with friends who were taking us to Atlanta. Now, THESE were true friends because true Georgians NEVER want to drive in Atlanta and most certainly NEVER want to go to Hartsfield International Airport!

We stood in line a LONG time to pick up the tickets that Dony and Reba had provided.

When we finally made it to the counter, the lady said,

> ***"Your bags are going to California, but you are not going to be able to catch this flight; it is boarding right now."***

She didn't KNOW Bill Jones!

We took off running, and I mean RUNNING! It was like something from a movie! The Atlanta airport is HUGE! We were forty-one years old, and Bill had health issues, so he eventually had to slow down. He was out-of-breath and pointing at me and yelling — in a scratchy voice

"Keep going! Keep going! Don't wait!"

I ran as fast as I could toward the appointed gate!

I saw the stewardess at the door, and she was calling LOUDLY.

"Jones? Jones?"

I tried to YELL, but I barely had enough air in my lungs to talk!

"HERE!!! We're here! We're COMING!"

I could not tell if she heard me or not, but Bill had a burst of energy and ran straight to the door, by-passing the stewardess! He stuck his foot in the door AS she was closing it.

"I'm sorry, Sir. This gate is closing."

"Not yet, it isn't!" exclaimed Bill.

Thank goodness it was 1996; we would be arrested today!

Now, here is where it gets funny!

A dear friend of ours who had a six-month-old baby had prepared a diaper bag filled with necessities. We had almost NOTHING of our own for a baby! We still had no definite assurance that we would return with a baby, so we didn't want to spend any of our money on the "dream." I had purchased a pretty baby blanket at a local store because I just couldn't resist. It hadn't been expensive, and I figured I could give it away at a baby shower if things fell through. I am trying to keep this real and not present myself as someone of GREAT FAITH when it came to this baby THING! I wasn't. I did KNOW that God was setting something up in California, and we needed to follow through, but I could not really imagine that we would come back with a baby.

Picture **THIS**!

By the time Bill and I got on the plane, it was fully loaded! The plane was full — except for our seats. Everyone was already seated and buckled in. No one was putting luggage away; no one was going to the bathroom. They were all just staring ahead at US as we burst into the cabin completely out of breath! I'm sure they had been wondering WHY the plane hadn't already taken off. The expressions on their faces told us that they were NOT too happy with the LATE comers — US!

I tell you; we were WHEEZING! We were middle-aged; we were carrying a DIAPER BAG, but we had NO BABY! We had to be a strange sight!

We grabbed our seats, buckled up, and sat there just trying to breathe. We were so breathless that we could not even talk for several minutes. I was afraid Bill might have a heart attack before we could even get off the ground! I was PRAYING!

We recounted that story many times and laughed about it! We couldn't imagine what those passengers must have thought about us. The lady who sat beside us didn't say much to us for the entire flight; I think she was scared of us! LOL!

So many miracles were about to happen in California! I could write an entire book just about that experience. I don't know if I will be able to fully describe to you in a couple of chapters all that God did! I desperately want to honor the magnitude of this miraculous experience.

Bill had warned me that we only had enough money for one week in San Jose, California, at the most! We had been told that the baby might arrive before we did, so we prayed during the entire flight that we would get there in time for the birth. To be able to be PRESENT at the baby's birth was such a GIFT! Our hearts were bursting at the thought of such a thing.

God provided! When we got off the plane in San Francisco, we had no idea who was going to meet us. We saw an older couple standing in the crowd holding up placards with Dony and Reba's picture on them! What a creative idea! They were a retired couple (Wendall and Marie) who attended the church where the revival was occurring. They had volunteered to house us in their beautiful condo for however long it took! They told us that they were going to take us wherever we needed to go during our time there. They also informed us that their church had agreed to provide meals for us during our stay. God was meeting every possible financial need right before our eyes! Every single thing that had concerned us was being taken care of. We had not asked anyone for help, but God knew every need, and He had gone before us to prepare the way!

These people were in a charismatic, nondenominational congregation. They didn't even know anything about our Pentecostal Holiness denomination. They didn't know US. They only knew that God was doing something wonderful, and they wanted to be a part of it. None of us could really know ALL that God was about to do; we were just along for the adventure of a lifetime!

Chapter Twenty-three

Baby Makes Three Part II

We were in California for a couple of weeks before the baby arrived; the doctor had miscalculated the due date! God used that time to allow us to meet the birth mom, to get to know Reba and Dony better, and to grow our own faith! We were taken care of completely and came back to Georgia with money in our pockets AND a baby! God did so much to our faith during that stay; He opened our eyes to the wide-eyed wonder of this beautiful congregation and how they worshipped so freely. These were well-educated, well-off techies for the most part. Many of them worked in the up-and-coming computer industry, and they were hungry and open to the moving of God's Spirit in their midst. We had never seen anything like it before, and it was a refreshing experience for us!

After two weeks of ANXIOUSLY waiting, the birth mom was admitted to the hospital on a Friday evening. Bill and I spent the night in the birthing suite with her. During the night, Bill snored softly on the little loveseat beside me, and the birth mom slept as the monitors kept a rhythm going in the room. She was not yet in labor, but they had begun to administer Pitocin to induce labor. They thought the baby was overdue at that point. There was NO WAY I was going to SLEEP! I was as nervous as a cat!

The birth mom had requested that we keep cassettes of Dony and Reba's music playing at all times. I would put a new cassette in when one finished playing. During the wee hours of Saturday morning something truly divine happened. God opened a supernatural window and allowed me to "see" His plan clearly, and there is no way that I can fully capture the majesty of that moment on paper.

About the time that we founded The Lighthouse, Bill had heard a song by Dony and Reba that spoke to him like no other! It was titled, "A People Who Were Not."

Sing those who were orphans, sing

Oh, Children of the Promise, Sing!

We who were not heirs, received adoption.

We cry, "Abba, Father; cry, "Abba, Father."

AND Sing those who were BARREN, Sing!

Travail in the Spirit, Sing!

Cause our husband, Christ,

He claimed us with His blood,

Oh, spiritual Israel, His Kingdom's borne.

And WE are that people who were NOT,

God's peculiar people who were not,

The seed of Abraham, sons of God

A chosen generation; a witness for all the world to see

We are that people; we ARE the people of God[1]

He asked me to learn the song, and he had me sing it over and over! I cannot tell you the number of times I sang that song in our services. Bill loved it because he felt it described our congregation. We had come from somewhere else; we were now a people who had NOT been a people before. We had started with nothing; we were barren. We had been adopted by the Father and become chosen for His purposes — a witness to those around us of God's love and grace!

I will tell you that EVERY time I sang that song, my heart broke just a bit. I was a BARREN woman, standing in front of a congregation, and singing about being barren. No one else may have thought of it THAT

1 Dony & Reba McGuire, K-Dimension

way, but I did. I am not even sure that Bill saw it that way at the time. I knew how much he loved the song, and it was a fitting song for our church, so I sang it.

In that dim hospital room in the wee hours of the morning, in the middle of Bill's soft snoring, and the sounds of the monitors, I suddenly became aware of Reba's voice.

> ***"Sing those who were BARREN, Sing..."***

As soon as the words played on the cassette player, God spoke to me!

> ***When Reba wrote the song, I knew...***
>
> ***Every time YOU sang the song, I knew...***
>
> ***Every time you dissolved in tears, I knew...***
>
> ***From the beginning of TIME, I knew...***
>
> ***That you would one day sit in this hospital room where your son WILL soon be born. I knew that you would hear this song! I knew that Reba had something to do with the unfolding of My miracle.***
>
> ***I knew... I ALWAYS knew...***

It was as if God pulled back the curtain of time and space and allowed me to understand ALL that He had done — the FULL plan! It was an indescribable moment for me, and there is simply no way for me to convey the supernatural impact of that revelation!

At the time, all I could do was sit on that hospital room loveseat and cry. Praise God for His love for me! Praise God for His plan that cut across time and space! Praise God for Reba's obedience to hear His prompting and call me that February afternoon! Praise God for this birth mom who was willing to go along with the plan of God! Praise God for this lovely California church who accepted us, loved us, and took care of us for almost three weeks! Praise God for Wendall and Marie who housed us and taxied us all over San Jose and San Francisco! It was more than I could really take in. I am still astounded to this day, and I am writing this through tears!

Reba wrote this on a card to our son after he was born. I have it in a box of other baby memorabilia.

Someday, you will understand how God moved Heaven and Earth to place you with your parents.

Blake Jones made his glorious entrance around 1:30 on Saturday afternoon. The mid-wife had just checked on things and started walking down the hallway.

The birth mom yelled, ***"He's coming!"***

Bill holding Blake 1st time

We ran into the hallway to get the mid-wife to come back. She only had time to get one glove on; the nurse was attempting to place the other one when baby Blake FELL out on a sheet! He came QUICKLY on the scene; no one was ready for him!

Bill was allowed to cut the cord. Blake was picked up in that same sheet and handed to ME. I was the first person to hold him. Several church members were in that hospital room with us. Reba was there (crying buckets), and her best friend, Judy, was videoing everything for us! Blake was born into this world with people praising God, crying and shouting, and praying in the Spirit!

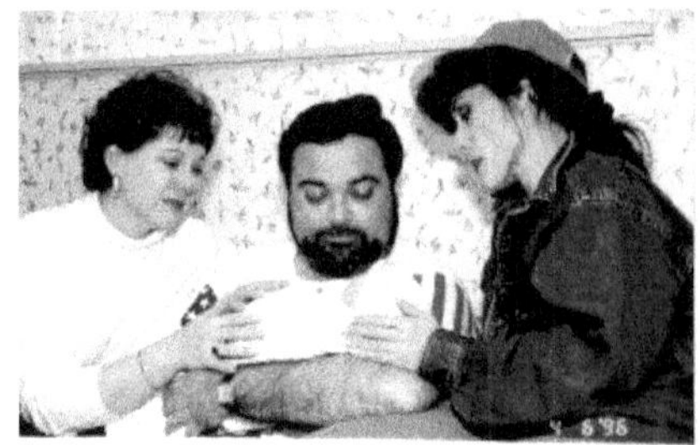

Karen, Bill, & Reba pray for Blake

Nurses from all over the hospital came by the room to see what was happening! Word spread like wildfire through the hospital that THIS was special; THIS was different! They wanted to see for themselves.

This hospital was noted for their innovative birthing facility. They gave Bill and me a beautiful dinner that night with special celebratory stemmed glasses for the occasion. When they came to discharge Blake, the nurse came in with a wheelchair. She looked at me and chuckled, and said, "Well, I guess you won't be needing THIS!" Someone in the room suggested that I should just go ahead and sit in the chair and hold Blake.

We took our baby out of the hospital eight hours after he was born. Wendall and Marie were there to take us back to the condo; the pastor's wife, and a dear couple from the church had stayed as well. They all helped us pack up things. Reba had gone shopping and had brought us a bag full of baby clothes. Blake was a little baby, and the outfit I used to take him out of the hospital just swallowed him whole! I will never forget the absolute joy of being wheeled down the corridor that night! People would stop and smile and look at the baby! I felt as if I were in a dream! It was surreal!

I could not help but exclaim as I was wheeled right up to the hospital entrance door.

> ***"This is unbelievable! We saw our baby born! Bill cut the cord, and I was the first one to hold him! We enjoyed the celebratory dinner from the hospital, and now I'm being wheeled out to the car with my baby in my arms! God has given us EVERYTHING but the PAIN!"***

The pastor's wife leaned down, put her face in front of mine, and spoke **TRUTH** into my heart.

> ***"God knew that you had ALREADY experienced the pain!***
>
> ***Nearly twenty-two years of it!"***

Two months after Blake's birth, Bill and I would celebrate our twenty-second wedding anniversary. Our friends had children who were going to college or getting married. We had shed untold amounts of tears as DECADES of infertility crushed us, as our dreams of being parents had been dashed over and over and over again.

Bill was most haunted by the many baby dedications he did over those twenty-two years. He shared with me that the devil had whispered in his ears over and over.

> ***Go ahead and dedicate somebody else's baby,***
> ***but YOUR arms are still empty!***

We had been denied the privilege of having our own biological children. That is a pain that would always be with us. I have never known the awe of feeling a child move in my womb or nurse at my breast. Bill and I never had the joy of feeling our baby kick inside of me. We could not look in our child's face and see familial resemblance to our relatives. That's just the way it is. I will say that now that Blake is a man, he does resemble Bill quite a bit. Isn't that just like God!

On the other hand, we witnessed a miracle of God that involved multitudes of people from sea to shining sea, and spanned decades of time. We experienced miracle after miracle!

- Dad Crawford's prophetic prayer (1975) about our son
- The prophetic prayer of a man we'd never met before at a Full-Gospel Businessmen's meeting in the 1980s
- Reba's prophetic prayer around 1990
- Reba's willingness to reach out to us after her vision in California
- The birth mother's willingness to carry Blake to term, to accept Reba's vision, and to place that sweet infant into our arms
- The people in Elberton who worked with us to get a home-study done in record time
- The lawyers on both coasts who were willing to give us discounted rates and allowed us to pay installments
- The doctor who overnighted us the document that proved Bill was healthy enough to be a parent
- The churches and individuals who came together and gave us money for the trip to California
- Dony and Reba's ministry who provided the plane tickets
- The plane that did NOT take off before we could get our feet in the door
- Wendall and Marie who housed us and taxied us everywhere
- The charismatic congregation who fed us, prayed for us, and walked this miraculous journey with us
- Having our one-day-old son being dedicated to the Lord in a beautiful church service in California with a packed church while he wore a stunning dedication gown hand-made by Dottie Rambo herself for Reba's children
- The well-known San Jose pediatrician — with a LONG waiting list — who agreed to see us after he heard the story. He had to give us written permission to take a three-day-old infant across the country on an airplane!

God could have worked a physical miracle and given us a biological baby. THAT is what we had prayed for and hoped for. The miracle He chose involved so many other people. It touched their lives in a way that a biological child of ours would not have. God's plan also gave Blake a loving father who would spend the rest of his life pouring godly guidance into him and changing the path of his life forever.

Prayers are never in vain, and tears are never wasted.

We carried that precious three-day-old infant across the country and back to Georgia. There are not enough words to describe how utterly exhausted and yet exhilarated we were. The stories we had to TELL! This was before social media, so most of our family and friends had no idea what God had done in California, but they would find out soon enough.

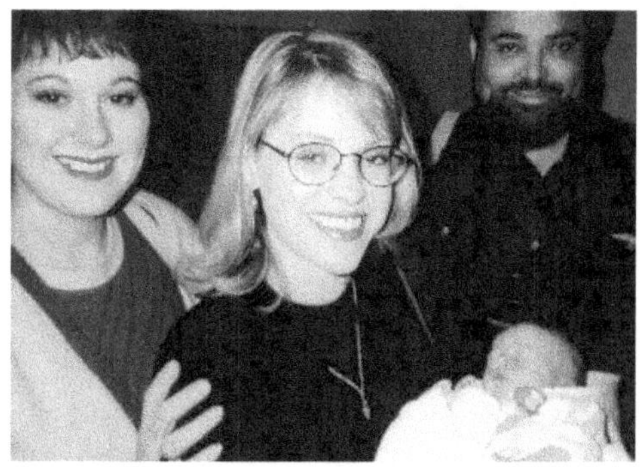

Sandy meets us at the airport

Sandy (my sister) was at the airport to meet us. She had flown in from Massachusetts to stay with us a few days and help me with the new baby. It was early in the wee hours of the morning when we drove into our little driveway to see our mailbox, the driveway, and our front porch COVERED in BLUE RIBBONS! What a delight! Bill's church office was also FILLED with blue ribbons and balloons.

God had not dropped a baby off on our porch in a basket tied with a bow, but he ***had*** dropped a promised son onto a sheet and into our arms, and he had friends decorate our home and our church with almost more blue bows than we could count! Believe me when I say that I got the message — loud and clear!

God's plan showed me that in my darkest moments of despair, He SAW me. He had the plan in place even though I could not see it. He loved me, and He was going to bless me in ways that I could not even dream of. Even when our hearts break, and we don't see the answers we desire, God's plan is always higher than ours. A favorite song of mine reminds us that when we can't see God's hands, we can **ALWAYS** trust His heart.

Georgia Baby Shower

Our church family, our neighbors, almost all of Elbert County, our family, and friends from around the globe seemed to be rejoicing with us. They had loved us through the heartache, and they were ready to laugh with us in the miracle of our son's birth.

Georgia Dedication

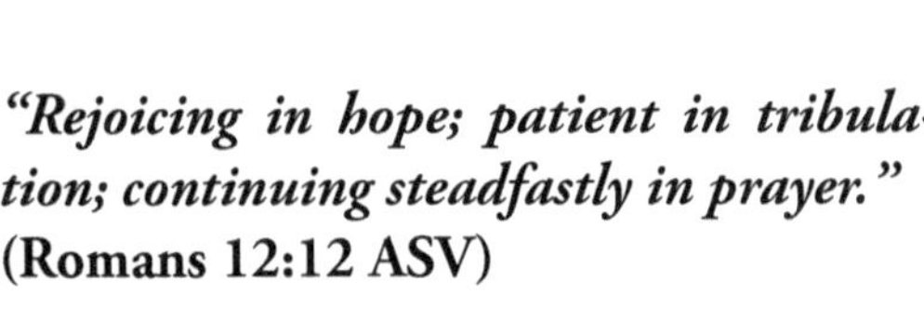

"Rejoicing in hope; patient in tribulation; continuing steadfastly in prayer."
(Romans 12:12 ASV)

Chapter Twenty-four

Seasons Shift

We were about to enter a new phase of our relationship — parenthood. It had come to us rather late, but it CAME! The baby stage was a delight for us! Bill and I shared everything equally. He would bathe Blake, change his diapers, get up in the night with him, play with him on the floor, and take him to the doctor. My heart aches for wives whose husbands will not help with their infants; I was blessed to have Bill's complete support. This was very new territory for me. I had never had much experience with infants, so I was a newbie! I will say that God gave me instant love for Blake and a willingness to do whatever needed to be done, but I was still incredibly grateful for Bill's fatherhood skills. He was a natural!

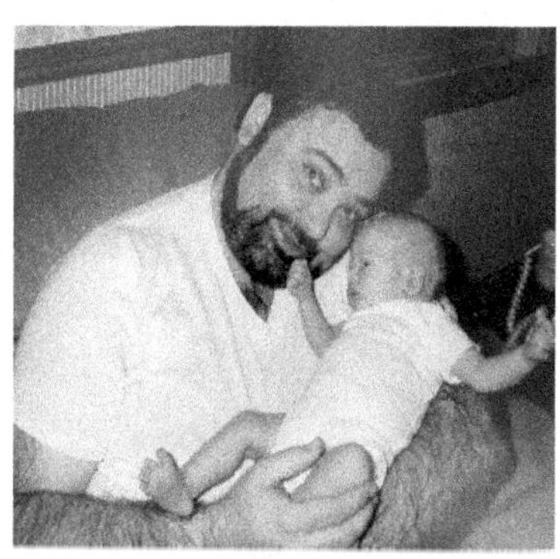

A Natural Father

Children always loved Bill! His size could have been intimidating, but his personality always calmed nerves. He would get down on a child's level and become his/her best friend. His nieces and nephews will testify to this; they all adored him! He would sing silly songs and make funny faces all day long! His giggle alone would endear him to children wherever he met them. They just sensed his love, and they loved him in return.

Enjoying Fatherhood

Having his own baby to tend was a delight for him! Blake was a happy and easy-going baby. He usually woke up happy and would entertain himself in his crib for a while before he wanted to get up. Bill would take me in his arms and snuggle me as we listened to Blake cooing in his crib. So many years of heartache made everything about loving a baby extra special to us, and we just basked in the joy of it all.

Blake on mower

I had watched young moms stroll their babies on the streets of Elberton for years. When the day came that I could put Blake in a stroller and walk down the street with him, I was beyond ecstatic! Strangers often thought that Blake was our grandchild which was understandable considering our ages. It really didn't offend us; we were just thrilled to be parents regardless. So many folks knew our story, and they were almost as happy as we were; it is simply a gross understatement to say that we enjoyed those baby years.Our later experiences would not be all that different from anyone else's- potty training, elementary programs, homework assignments, ballgames, teen angst and rebellion, jobs, and graduations. We tackled them head on just like everyone else. We shed our tears; we stayed on our knees, and we did the best we could. We made mistakes; we made plenty of them, but we did the best we knew how to do. That's all any parent can do.

Family Portrait

I believe we appreciated the experience more than most because we fought incredibly hard for the privilege of being parents. Nothing about it came easily for us. People always appreciate what they fight for, and some things in life are WORTH the fight.

In June of 1998 when Blake was only two years old, Bill was named Elberton's Father of the Year in the local paper, *The Elberton Star*. I wrote the nominating letter, and I was so happy when Bill won the competition!

Dear Elberton Star:

A couple of weeks ago, my husband twisted his knee as he was mowing our lawn. He used a cane for a day or two and suffered for about another week with a sore knee and stiff calf muscle. Our two-year-old son noticed that Daddy was having some difficulty, and it seemed to concern him. I told him to go and kiss Daddy's knee and pray for it. He happily ran over to where his dad reclined on the floor and leaned down to plant a typically sloppy toddler kiss on the injured knee. He then proceeded to "pray." He simply said, "Jeezzus, bwess Daddy's knee." My husband looked up at me with huge tears in his eyes, grabbed our little boy into his arms, and cried. My heart was filled with love and admiration for this man who loves his son so completely.

I believe that my husband, Bill Jones, deserves to be named Father of the Year for many reasons. After waiting almost twenty-two years for the joys of fatherhood, Bill does not take it for granted. He sacrifices his time and his privacy to care for our son, Blake, whenever possible. For several months, he worked during the afternoons and evenings so that Blake would only have to attend day care for two days a week. He willingly exhausted himself in the best interest of his son.

Bill loves to make up songs on the spot — none of which are musically worthy to be printed here. (Sorry, Honey) The good thing is that Blake couldn't care less! I have the honor of doing a lot of singing around Elberton, but I have to admit that Blake prefers Daddy's singing to mine. I try not to take it personally, but the hardest pill to swallow is when Blake wants me to sing the songs that Bill has made up.

For so many years my heart was broken as I saw my husband yearn for children that we could not have. As a pastor, he has held many babies and dedicated them to the Lord, and I knew

> ***that — secretly — his heart was breaking for a baby of his own. Fatherhood is an awesome experience for anyone, but for a man such as my husband, the joy is boundless.***
>
> ***Bill Jones is Father of the Year in our house every day! He shines as an example of a godly father. Blake will grow up knowing what it is to be loved and honored. He is too young to nominate his daddy, so I am happy to do it for him. As Bill's son, Blake is the true winner; his dad is the best!***

That June also brought BIG changes in our lives when Bill was offered a full-time position in our conference leadership. He would need to give up pastoring The Lighthouse in order to cover the state of Georgia in the areas of Evangelism, Missions, and Church Planting.

There had been many times along the way when I hoped Bill would be able to leave the stresses of pastoring a local church. This was NOT one of those times! I struggled with this shift in our lives. Blake was just a toddler, and I wanted him to grow up in The Lighthouse! Our congregation was incredibly loving and supportive, and a large part of our church family had been with us through so many of our hard times and heartaches. Several families had loved us and ministered alongside us since we arrived in Elberton in 1978. They had helped us start The Lighthouse and had been faithful to that ministry for fourteen years. They were like family to us; we felt their complete support, and I did not want to leave. Bill struggled with leaving also, but he was feeling the call of God.

Some may find this hard to believe, but Bill had never had aspirations for conference leadership. He was a gifted pastor who LOVED pastoring, and he was always committed to his congregations. He once told me that wherever God sent him, he was THERE until he died unless God changed his course. That proved to be true in every situation.

We prayed sincerely for God's will. Bill told me that he felt God was opening a door for him to minister in this new position; he sensed God directing him into a larger area of leadership. His salary would increase; I won't deny that we both liked that reality, but it was **NOT** the driving force. We lived in our own home, and our church was supporting us well. I enjoyed my teaching job in Elberton, and I did not want to change jobs either. We didn't have lots of extras, but we were living comfortably at the time.

I knew that Bill would be on the road a lot more. Most men in Bill's position had grown children; their wives traveled with them most of the time. I knew that I could not always go with him since Blake was only two. I was concerned about a lack of stability for our little boy. Having such a young child would definitely complicate things.

After a time of much prayer and even more discussion, I knew that God was changing our direction. I trusted Bill's guidance; I always had. I had never wanted to stand in his way, and this was an exciting opportunity for us, but it wasn't without some angst on my part.

Saying goodbye to our beloved Lighthouse folks was so hard. Many tears were shed on the Sunday Bill announced that he would be stepping down. We had a portrait made and gave it to the church. They loved on us and sent us away with a blessing, and God eventually led us back to them. They were and will ALWAYS be family to us.

Leaving The Lighthouse

We put our house up for sale; Bill knew we needed to distance ourselves a bit so that a new pastor would have a chance. We bought a new home in Colbert which is about thirty minutes away from Elberton. At the time we were still using landlines, and it was long-distance to call from Elberton to Colbert! Bill wanted it that way; he was so wise. He didn't want our church folks to keep calling Pastor Bill for advice when they needed to be building relationship with their new pastor. I was able to commute to Elberton and keep my teaching job for a few more years. We were also close to Athens Christian School where we planned to send Blake when he was old enough. Bill's commute to the conference office in Franklin Springs was about twenty-five minutes, so everything fell into place pretty well.

Colbert is a very small town, and we have absolutely loved living here. God provided another beautiful home for us; it had also been repossessed! When we gave the real estate agent our best offer, she laughed at us. She thought we were joking! She had never met the Budget King! Once again, we watched God move on our behalf; he gave us the house of our dreams at a price none of you would believe. He also gave us the best neighbors on the planet! We have been surrounded by loving and caring neighbors for the past twenty-seven years. That gave Bill peace of mind when he was gone for weeks at a time.

Bill had been serving as assistant to the conference superintendent since 1994, and he was re-elected to that position in 1998. When the conference superintendent, Dr. Doug Beacham, was elected to serve as a national leader in 2001, Bill stepped into the position of conference superintendent to finish out the term which greatly increased his scope of responsibility. It was a huge step for him and for us.

Exciting changes were in the air for us, but one change was coming which placed us on yet another collision course with death. Once again, kidney failure came knocking at our door, and we had no choice but to answer.

Chapter Twenty-five

Not AGAIN!

Bill's second occurrence of kidney failure did not come as such a shock. He had been having regular check-ups with kidney specialists since 1982. His creatinine levels began to slowly climb, and we knew what that meant. Creatinine is a waste product in the blood that is removed by the kidneys. When kidney function declines, the creatinine levels rise. It is a main indicator of kidney failure. Evelyn's kidney had given Bill an extra nineteen years of life! What a phenomenal blessing that was to us!

Bill did not want to go on dialysis again. He also told me that he would not bring a dialysis machine into the house this time. As depressing as the clinics were, he said that when we were dialyzing at home, he could never get away from it! The chair, the machine, and the room filled with supplies were a constant reminder of his weakened state. He wanted another transplant, and the search for a new kidney donor went into high gear!

Bill's siblings had gotten older, and none of them were able to donate this time. My family still didn't qualify because of blood type. Bill was forty-seven years old now; his chances of getting a cadaver transplant (for a second kidney transplant) were not good. All we could do was pray, and everyone we knew was agreeing with us for another miracle!

Blake was only five years old when Bill got sick again. We tried not to scare him with what was happening. Bill began to experience all of the weakness and sickness that he had the first time. He was retaining fluids; his face got puffy. His breathing was labored, and his energy level was low. He tried to pretend that he felt better than he did, but I knew. I knew.

One night I couldn't sleep. Bill was snoring very heavily due to his difficulty breathing. His kidney just could not keep up with fluid levels in his body which was scaring me. I quietly got out of bed and went upstairs to check on Blake. I looked at our little boy sleeping peacefully in his bed, unaware that he might be losing his daddy.

I walked down the upstairs hallway and sat down on the top step and completely lost it!

I had been holding my emotions in check, but it all came to a head that night. I pleaded with God! I cried out to Him with all I had within me!

> ***"God! If Bill dies now, Blake will not really remember him! I want him to grow up KNOWING his daddy! I want Bill's influence to be felt in his life. You gave us this little boy in such a miraculous way; please don't take his daddy away now. Please God! You have done so much for us, and I'm asking You again! Hear my prayers! Please hear my prayers! Make a way! We need another miracle, Lord. One more! Please!"***

I had witnessed so many miracles in my life! I felt guilty asking for ONE MORE! What was my miracle allotment? Had I crossed the line into selfishness? As all of these thoughts and emotions raced for first place in my brain, I just kept begging God for MORE! ONE MORE MIRACLE, LORD! I could not stop myself. I didn't want to lose Bill, and I especially didn't want Blake to lose him! The emotions had to be expressed, and in that dark moment on the top of the stairs, I released them to my Lord. We serve a God who loves us when we are at our worst, when we are broken, and when we are needy. I felt like the poster child for all of those categories that night, but I knew God saw me. I knew that He would be with me — no matter what happened.

One of our dear friends had volunteered to be tested as a possible donor, and we were hopeful. Finally, we had some light at the end of this dark tunnel! Our hopes were crushed when some family members expressed concerns, and she felt she had to back out. When someone is offering to undergo surgery and give you a life-giving organ, you learn to tread softly. It must be their choice; you cannot apply any pressure. We were disappointed, but we knew she loved us, and we knew she felt conflicted. We kept praying, and praying…and praying. So many sleepless nights filled with prayer as Bill continued to decline.

We were thrilled when our old friend, Billy Griffin, said he would like to be tested! Wow! Hope rose in us once again. Paula called the hospital in Augusta and started setting things in place for Billy's testing. During the conversation, Paula casually asked the nurse if she could be tested. She was taking some medication which she thought might hinder her chances of maybe being a donor. The nurse said that was not a problem at all, so Paula asked to be tested as well. It was exciting for us to know that both of them were going to be tested; it would increase the odds of at least one match.

When the results came in, Paula was an excellent match; Billy was not. My best friend since the age of four was willing to donate a kidney to my beloved Bill. My heart was humbled by such a gift. We told her multiple times that she didn't have to do this. Her response was always the same.

"I know that. I'm doing it because I WANT to do it."

Things began to move quickly with a myriad of tests. This meant multiple trips back and forth to doctor's offices for Paula and for us. Bill and I also felt such gratitude that Billy, along with their two children, Amy and Jonathan, supported Paula's decision. They did not stand in the way of the kidney transplant, and they deserved our love and gratitude as well.

Unbelievably, Bill faced a conference election in June of 2002. He and Paula were in the final stages of preparation for a transplant operation which was scheduled for July. Bill was sick, and it was showing on him at this point. He was pale and weak. He had been filling the position of superintendent since 2001, but he needed to be elected by the conference in session to continue serving. We were facing the very real possibility that he could lose this election. It was understandable that they might not want to elect him to serve a four-year term in his condition. If he did not survive the surgery, they would be faced with having to elect someone else.

Six Days before 2nd Transplant

When election time came, the conference showed great love, respect, and honor for Bill when they elected him to serve as the superintendent of the conference for a four-year term. They knew he was very sick; they knew what he was facing, but their faithfulness to him spoke volumes.

On July 10, 2002, I watched as my nearly life-long best friend was rolled down the hall to go to her side of an adjoining surgical suite. I also saw Bill being rolled into the other surgical suite. Kidney transplants are performed frequently these days, and they are probably considered much less risky than other transplant surgeries. Bill always said that it is ONLY minor surgery when it is being done on someone else! He was right about that. I have known serious complications to result from "simple" procedures, so we must always take any surgery seriously.

For this transplant surgery, I had several family members and friends with me at the hospital. I appreciated the support, but I will never forget the way my heart felt when I knew what was going on behind those closed doors. I could possibly lose my husband AND my best friend on the same day. That was quite a lot to process.

Best Friends

The transplant operation was a huge success! Bill's recovery from this transplant was even quicker than the first! They were managing his pain levels much better this time. Medicine is always improving and methods get better over time.

Bill suffered so much over his adult lifetime. I once asked him how he could keep a good attitude about all of the procedures, the office visits, and the medications. He said he just looked at it as mountains he had to climb. Climb one mountain and enjoy the view, then climb the next mountain, and the next. He said that he was "buying time." If he lived long enough, methods would improve, and they would have a better answer for him! That was his philosophy.

Bill was a FIGHTER — a WARRIOR! He valued life, and the man fought to live! He was relentless in that fight. I know he became weary with the battle, but he would not surrender to it; he would not give up. He kept climbing those mountains and buying time, and I'm so glad he did.

My man had beaten death once again. He got stronger, and he kept ministering. He was older now, and two kidney transplant operations had taken a toll on him. As tough as he was, the battles were getting harder with each passing year.

This second kidney would last him almost twenty-three years. The effects of the anti-rejection medications began to take their toll. I remembered what the doctor had told me in Augusta so many years ago. He was right. Bill had to take the medications to prevent rejection, but the meds created an entirely new set of challenges for him and MANY more mountains to climb.

Chapter Twenty-six

Too Many Mountains

Let me take this chapter to just fill you in on some of the other health challenges that Bill faced. If I tried to detail each one, I would need to write about five other books, so this will be a sort of "in a nutshell" chapter for you.

- In 1994, Bill was diagnosed with adult-onset diabetes and began taking insulin shots.
- In 1998, they discovered an aneurysm at his old dialysis graft site and surgery was performed.
- Diabetes worsened in 2002, probably as a result of his meds. Insulin injections were increased.
- In 2005 he had back surgery (lumbar laminectomy)
- In December of 2006 he had his first squamous cell skin cancer removed.
- In April of 2008, Bill suffered his first heart attack.
- In 2011 he was hospitalized with a serious case of cellulitis in his arm.
- 2013 brought gall bladder surgery into the picture.
- Bill also began using an insulin pump in 2013.

That is just a "snapshot" covering quite a few medical issues along the way. As serious as they were, something hit Bill that was far more serious in 2015.

It was a train. Yep! A train.

Bill wasn't actually hit by the train, but his truck was.

Bill returned to Elberton to pastor in January 2015. After seventeen years away in full-time conference ministry, we returned to pastor the church we had founded. It was no longer The Lighthouse; they had changed the name to Celebration Outreach Center during the tenure of another pastor. The name was different, but it still felt like home.

We never expected to return to pastoral ministry, but God had other plans. Bill always desired to follow God, and he had a great vision for the church and was anxious to get back into the trenches. I had determined from the very beginning of our relationship that I would support Bill and do all I could to stand by him in ministry. This time was no different. At the time we thought it was for what WE could bring to the church, but we discovered that God had taken us home because we were going to NEED our church family. We were going to need them as never before.

On Wednesday night, October 28, 2015, Bill was returning home from his Wednesday night Bible Study. I had not been attending Wednesday nights because I was teaching at Athens Christian by that time. I worked late most days and just did not have the time to drive to Elberton on a school night. I was expecting Bill home at any moment when the phone rang.

> ***"Honey, I've had an accident. My car went in a ditch; they want to check me out. Come on to the hospital."***

I tried to question him further, but he said he had to go. His voice sounded strange; I couldn't figure out why, but I quickly left for Elberton. When I approached the outskirts of town, I saw fire trucks and police cars lined up on the left-hand side of the four-lane beside the railroad tracks. A train was stopped there also. My heart began to race inside of my chest. Surely not! I had pictured his truck being "in the ditch" at a different location. I could not let myself believe that Bill was involved in THIS!

Upon arriving at the hospital, I asked to see my husband. I explained that he had been in an accident.

Another nurse walked by and said, ***"He's the one from the train wreck."***

Bill was approaching a stop sign at the edge of a four-lane (five counting the turn lane in the middle). We still are not sure what happened, but his truck went into a skid and would not stop. He went across all five lanes and ended up on the edge of the train tracks. He was in a state of shock when the truck stopped moving. This particular set of tracks is quite busy; we would see trains every day. He said he had only one thought at the time.

"Thank God there's no train!"

At that very moment, he heard the whistle blow!

He knew he was hurt, but he had to get out of the truck. It wasn't squarely on the tracks, but he still knew the train would make contact. He was able to get the door open and get out. A policeman had actually witnessed Bill's truck skidding across the road and had called for help.

Bill's Truck

Truck's Steering Wheel

He asked Bill if he could get back up the incline, and Bill said he didn't think he could. He was able to get out of the way enough before the train passed.

The train clipped the truck just enough to knock off the hood and send it flying like a Frisbee in the air! The frame was bent terribly, and the truck was completely totaled. When a train and truck collide; the train wins every single time.

Bill's chest had hit the hard steering column. The hard truck steering wheel was bent like it had been made of clay. Bill's sternum was cracked, and he had six broken ribs; the pain was excruciating. He was transported via ambulance the next day to Augusta. His injuries were serious, and they wanted him there to be closely watched by the kidney specialists.

The ER trauma doctor came to see me while Bill was in Augusta. His comments didn't surprise me at all.

> ***"Mrs. Jones, your husband is a BEAST! We have a thirty-five-year-old man with fewer internal injuries, and he can barely move. Your husband is doing far more! We are astounded, frankly!"***

I asked him if he had looked over Bill's medical history. He said that he had. None of the doctors could fathom how Bill could survive and keep going. There is only one explanation. God. That's it. God.

This accident did change things for Bill. He had a truly difficult time with recovery once we got him home. I had no idea how hard it would be for Bill; he had been such a trouper with every other surgery and medical emergency. My daddy called me and said that I would probably need Mama to come and stay with us for a while; I had not even considered needing help, but —have mercy— did I EVER need help! When we got home from the hospital, it took me forty-five minutes to get Bill from the garage to the bedroom. He was in such pain and so crippled from the wreck! When I began to understand how weak he was, I started to doubt his ability to recover.

Bill's older brother, Floyd Jr., stayed with us for a week. He built a small platform to help Bill get into the bed. He encouraged Bill to move as much as he could, which helped greatly with his recovery. Bill would NEVER have done that for me, but this was BIG BROTHER (a high school coach at one time), and he would NOT resist him! Thank God for a big brother when we needed one! Mama stayed for about a month! She kept an eye on Bill while I was at school each day. She also cooked a little bit for us which was a great help. Mama was beginning to show signs of the dementia, which would take her from us in nine short years. I saw things that concerned me while she was with us, so I didn't ask her to do much. I just wanted her to watch out for Bill and notify me if a problem arose. I thank God that Daddy saw what I needed even when I did not.

That wreck marked the beginning of true decline for Bill. He began to experience AFib episodes in early 2016, and his cardiologist indicated that the impact to his chest in that wreck may have precipitated it. He continued to struggle with AFib episodes, and he also began having reduced lung capacity after the wreck. There is no doubt that this accident severely impacted his health for the rest of his life.

Over the years he had multiple heart caths and ablation procedures. He had multiple stents placed in his heart. In 2017 he developed a very large hematoma on his upper left leg following an ablation. He suffered quite a bit with it before being informed that they had punctured an artery and a vein during the ablation. He had multiple appointments from September through December due to internal bleeding from that procedure.

On August 2, 2018, Bill had another heart attack. This time it was ventricular tachycardia. His doctor told me that this was the BAD type of heart attack. Bill had made me drive him to the hospital. (Bill had driven himself to the hospital for his first heart attack. Remember, the man was a BEAST.) The cardiologist told him never to do that again.

They implanted a pacemaker defibrillator on August 3.

Bill had yet another heart attack on March 17, 2021. He was suffering from congestive heart failure by this time.

Over the next few years there were too many doctor visits and hospitalizations to count or to list here. His meds were changed as often as I changed the sheets on our bed. He had cataract surgeries on both eyes; thankfully they went well. Bill signed up to be an organ donor; a cause that is dear to our hearts. I can still remember him saying this:

> ***"I'm such a mess. The only thing I will probably be able to donate will be my eyes!"***

In the spring of 2023, the cardiology team told him that they were unable to attempt any new treatments for the AFib. He did have one more heart catheterization from a new cardiologist in November of 2023. She wanted Bill to try for a heart transplant. He was against it, and so was I. We knew what that would entail, and Bill didn't believe he was strong enough for it. He wanted to be home with me and Blake for as long as he could, and he wanted to have his freedom, so that is what we did.

Bill held his own from November 2023 until July 2025. He had good days and bad days, but his kidney function stayed strong. He truly did better than anyone expected, and our lives settled into an easy rhythm.

Preaching in Wheelchair

We spent our days at home. Bill had been using a walker for a while; mobility was difficult. We would go to doctor's appointments and to church on most Sunday mornings. There were a few Sundays when Bill didn't feel up to it, but not many. When my mom passed away in July of 2024, my daddy loaned us her wheelchair. Bill liked using it at church because he could wheel himself to the front to pray for people when he felt led. He would preach from the wheelchair when Pastor John Case asked him to fill in. Bill had stepped down as lead pastor on Sunday, September 25, 2022. Pastor John grew up under Bill's ministry, and what a divine appointment it was when Bill prayed for him and passed the mantle of ministry to him. We dearly loved this congregation, and we loved and had confidence in Pastor John. We both felt God's peace in that moment.

Bill didn't rest easily anymore, so I would let him sleep as long as he wanted. During the last year of his life, he would often sleep until 11:00 or so. He told me that he had his best sleep during those late morning hours. He would move to his recliner in the living room and turn on the news. I would fix him something to eat. Later on, he would switch to "Wagon Train" or "Gunsmoke" for a few hours. Sometimes we would find something to watch together, and that was always nice. It was our daily routine, and we just enjoyed being together, breathing the same air together, HAVING each other.

When Bill was doing well, he loved going to movies with me. It was always one of our favorite things. When Blake was growing up, we often went to movies together and loved it! In the later years, it helped when Blake would go with us to help Bill navigate steps. During his last months, he stopped mentioning going to the movies, and I didn't request it. It just took too much effort and energy.

Every moment together was precious — a gift. We never took those moments for granted.

This short chapter has been filled with FAR too many medical diagnoses and treatments. It may have been difficult for you to read it.

That's why I included it. This…THIS was Bill's life. This was OUR life together. We had eight years of normalcy before the medical nightmares began. We just did what we had to do. It was never what we wanted to do. It was never the life we wanted to live. Some folks would say it was the cards we were dealt, but I don't like that expression.

> ***"I have told you these things, so that in me you may have peace. In this world you will have trouble. But take heart! I have overcome the world."***
> **(John 16:33 NIV)**

We live in a fallen world; there is disease in this life. There is suffering in this life. Some folks have more pain and suffering than others. Bill's life was hard, and as his wife — joined as one flesh — so was mine. Through every trial, and in the midst of all the suffering, God was with us.

Without the difficulties, we would not have witnessed the miracles.

Chapter Twenty-saven

Bubba Yu

You already know that God gave us our son through a miraculous series of events, but you haven't read about our "other" son. I could not write a book about our journey without including our "Chinese son." That's what we call Yubo Yu.

Facebook Post by Karen: August 22, 2015

I went to sleep praying for my boys and woke up praying for my boys. I was also remembering...

Nothing in my life (outside of salvation) has changed me more than being a mom. Blake was the sweetest and easiest baby anyone could ask for; I adored the privilege of being his mommy. I thought our nest was full, and I was satisfied, but God wasn't.

Adolescence with Blake was not an easy journey; many of you can relate to that. Remember that we hit that stage when our friends were beginning to retire and relax! It was during a particularly difficult place (not long after my sister died) that God sent Yubo Yu into our family. Oh yes, he was sent by God; we would not have added another teen-aged boy to the mix if it hadn't been God! Ask Bill Jones about it; he will agree! God convinced me first; it took Bill awhile longer to come around! Yubo is not our legally adopted son; his family lives in China, but he is definitely a "son" in our

hearts. He came to us when he and Blake were both fourteen. They graduated Athens Christian High School last May, and we love each of them beyond words.

Yubo and Blake

Blake and Yubo have very different personalities, and they could both be quite difficult in their own ways. They got along like real brothers which meant they were either beating each other up and tearing up the house or laughing like silly school girls and conniving together about something! They kept me either laughing OR crying about something nearly all the time.

I know this has been a LONG post, and here is my point: God's miraculous provision in our lives may come with some difficulties along the way. Being a mom to Blake and Yubo has not always been an easy journey; in fact, it has been quite stressful at times. Even though we have had many bumps in the road (or potholes), I would not trade my motherhood for anything in the world. I learned that children are trained by us, but they are not held captive by us. They have free wills, and they make choices. Some of those choices are not always wise, but we hope and pray that our children will learn from their mistakes as much as we learn from our own. The boys have taught me more than I've ever taught them. I saw my own faults and failures much more clearly through their eyes. God has used them to strengthen my faith along the way.

Bill and I are "empty nesters" now. I just wanted you to know that we spent the first twenty-two years of our marriage alone. We are alone again, but we have been changed by parenthood. Every parent is changed by his/her children. Thank you, Lord, for allowing me to be a mom to Blake and then to Yubo. Thank you for allowing me to experience the late-night feedings, the scraped elbows and knees, "Santa Claus" and "Tooth Fairy" imaginings, the "Birds and the Bees" discussion, football games with Blake, soccer games with Yubo, school plays, graduations, and dorm room

preparations. There were times when I didn't think I could make it, but You gave me the strength to make it a day at a time, and I "wouldn't take nothin' for my journey now."

Yubo came to us as a foreign exchange student from China during his freshman year of high school. He was just a few months younger than our son, Blake. We were knee-deep in adolescent "issues" with Blake, so we were NOT looking for another teen-ager at the time! Bill was serving in denominational leadership and traveling quite a bit. We were BUSY folks! Our school (Athens Christian School) would regularly present opportunities for families to house exchange students, but I had never even considered it UNTIL I saw the e-mail about Yubo.

God has a unique way of getting our attention if we are open to His Spirit. I kept reading that e-mail, and I knew that God was speaking to me. I quickly e-mailed Bill at the conference office and told him that I thought we should consider taking this boy.

He responded quickly with this deeply thoughtful and spiritual response.

"Have you lost your mind?"

Later on, we would chuckle about that response! I was not derailed; I told him to pray about it. It wasn't long before he got back to me and said we would at least look into it. As you have already seen, sometimes God would get my attention first and then use me to help bring Bill along! Bill often said that it was especially aggravating when the Holy Spirit's voice sounded just like ME!

Yubo's adjustment to an American family was not always easy. He had never attended church in his life until we took him. He had no real concept of Christianity. Our home was strict in areas where he had been given freedom in China. Bless his heart! We told him that we wouldn't ask him to do anything that we didn't ask Blake to do. We wanted him to be part of our family — not a guest in our home. It wasn't always easy, but that is exactly what happened; Yubo became FAMILY.

Family Complete

Thankfully, Yubo is a pretty flexible and easy-going guy. We did find out that IF something really mattered to him, he would stand Bill nose-to-nose and be defiant! We had a stand-off after a few months, and I thought that Yubo would have to go back to China. I was PRAYING hard and crying buckets because Yubo had already become a "son" in my heart. I didn't want to lose him! Praise God that Yubo's father in China intervened and instructed Yubo to "when in Rome, do as the Romans do." Yubo relented, and the crisis was averted! Thank God for answered prayers!

Bill with his boys

Once things settled down, Yubo truly did become part of our family. He started calling me, "Mother," and he still does, but he says it in his Chinese accent, and it comes out as "Motha." I LOVE it! Bill said he would have to make Yubo "southern," so he nicknamed him, "Bubba Yu." Yubo absolutely adores southern fried chicken, so I think he loved his southern nickname as well.

God brought this young man into our family, and I give Him praise for that. Before he flew back to China for the summer after his first year here, Yubo accepted Jesus as His Savior! He didn't want to leave without Jesus in His heart. He was also baptized before he graduated high school, and Bill was able to baptize him. What a wonderful day that was for our entire family!

We were never able to have biological children, but God gave us two sons in very different ways. Look, Folks, we couldn't have dreamed up these scenarios on our own! We serve a creative God for sure!

Yubo has been away from us for many years now, but he stays in touch as much as he can. He dreams of getting a job in the United States so that he can be closer to us. That is certainly my prayer as well. I know that if God wants him here, He will open a door and make a way. I will always be thankful for the four years that we were able to pour into Yubo's life and for the years of joy he has given to us. He will ALWAYS be part of our family.

Facebook Post by Bill: May 17, 2015

Blake's and Yubo's HS Graduation

Yubo Yu, Our Chinese "son" graduated from Athens Christian School last evening. Yubo is an exchange student who has lived in our home for the last three and a half years. We are so proud of him. Our hearts are aching in that he will fly back to China on tomorrow morning. We are glad that he has come to know Christ while living in our home and we trust that he will serve Christ wherever the Lord leads him.

Chapter Twenty-eight

No Filters

We live in an age of social media and photo filters. We can make ourselves as smooth and shiny as we want and put all our business out for everyone to view. We can paint a pretty picture and no one sees the mess in our lives.

I promised to be honest in the Prologue, and I have done my best to do just that, but I'm not quite finished. Bill Jones and I had a love that was deep and strong. Our relationship was special — at least to us. We also saw multiple miracles in our fifty-one years together. I wrote this book because I want our story to inspire others even after we both are gone.

There is a flip side, and to be totally honest, I need to share it also.

Back during that summer of 1973 when we were young and so passionately in love, we were both as blind as bats regarding each other. That's typical of "new" love no matter how old the couple might be. The "feel good" hormones rise, and we just can't see beyond the fog they create. In June of 2019, I did a series on marriage myths during my "Teachable Moments" on Sunday mornings. I will explain more about those "Moments" later. The myth for one of those was "My Spouse is Perfect." I shared this paragraph from one of my letters to Bill.

Letter from Karen August 23, 1973

My Dearest, Darling Billy,

I was telling Mama today how perfectly matched we are. No joke! I tried to think of something I didn't like about you, and I couldn't think of ONE thing. I love everything about you. I can't think of ANY faults that you have — in my sight. You have faults, I'm sure. Everybody does, but so far, you've done a good job of keeping them from me. I could never see me with anyone else now because you are PERFECT for me. No one else could meet your standards. I love you so very, very, very, very much!!!!

I will confess that I CRINGE now when I read that paragraph! When I found that letter and read through it in preparation for my Teachable Moment, I could not stop laughing! Tears ran down my face as I struggled to breathe. I took it downstairs and read it to Bill in the midst of my laughter. For some reason he didn't find it as funny as I did! LOL! I guess you have figured out by now that Bill DID have some faults, and so did I; it just took a little while for the "new" to wear off before we could see them.

Jones Siblings at Topsail Island

In the very first chapter of this book, I told you that Bill was the baby of five children, and I was the firstborn of three. If you know anything about birth order, you may recognize that we were destined to butt heads at times! I am a "get-er-done" type of person, and Bill was certainly spoiled as the baby of the family. His brother is closest in age, and he was eight years older than Bill. His three sisters treated him as if he were THEIR baby which is normal. He was doted on for sure!

I wanted things done MY way (always the BEST way), and he EXPECTED me to do things HIS way! We used to laugh at how his sisters would hide him to keep him from getting a spanking when he was little. I was the one telling on Sandy and Barry and HOPING they would get a spanking! I definitely thought I was the "boss of them," and Barry still accuses me of that today!

To summarize, Bill Jones and I could FIGHT with the best of them! The man was as stubborn as they come, and he had a temper. I happen to be quite independent, and I was not always the quiet, little, obedient wife. I would talk back and sometimes — just say, "No." He wasn't accustomed to that, so it caused quite a bit of friction at times.

Christmas 2009
(Last one with Sandy)

Years ago, we had a church family move behind us. Bill and I were both concerned that they would hear us fighting because we could get LOUD! We were passionate folks; that's the way we were. We loved passionately, and we could fight passionately!

Neither of us ever became physical, but we both WANTED to smack each other from time to time! (Just joking — sort of!) I often told my students that the thing that kept us together during a fight was that I had a car and a credit card! I could leave the house for a few hours and let us both cool off. By the time I came home, Bill was human again, and I had more patience with him. How's THAT for some honesty!

In other words, Folks, we were just a NORMAL couple. We were not saints who walked around in our Sunday best every day smiling at each other and being sweet. He had bad days, and so did I. He could be too demanding, and I could be too pushy. He would do anything for the church, but I had a really hard time getting him to do things at home. It's like the carpenter who won't fix his own cabinets, or the mechanic whose car is on blocks in the back yard! Bill would tell me to stop nagging him, and I would tell him to just do "it" already!

Like many pastors, Bill had difficulty separating church "work" from God. An example of that was when I was named 1996 Elbert County Teacher of the Year. It was a huge deal to me; I had not won a lot of awards in my life. I could have been the poster child for "Second Place" or "1st Runner-up." Bill had won MANY awards in his lifetime.

Teacher of the Year

The county was paying for us to go to the statewide dinner where all the county winners would be recognized. I can't remember now, but the dinner may have been in Macon that year. I was so excited about us getting to spend a night at a hotel and to enjoy a nice banquet together! Bill informed me that he would not be able to go because he had agreed to perform a small private wedding that Saturday. This couple did not attend our church; Bill just knew the family. The father was a minister also. The wedding was very small—family only—and it was not a formal affair. I asked Bill to check with them about changing the date.

> ***"You really want me to ask them to change the date of their wedding so I can attend a banquet with you?"***

I knew the battle was lost. He did not see the importance of the banquet to me. I did my best to convince him, but I got nowhere. I had to drive to this hotel alone — without GPS or a cell phone. I stayed in that room —alone. I went to the banquet—alone. I accepted my recognition without anyone to cheer me on. It was a hard night for me; I was hurt by his choice. I felt he should have put me first in that situation. Instead of enjoying this very special event in my life, I spent it sad and alone. Maybe I was wrong; maybe I was selfish. I only know I felt he chose them over me on an occasion when I wanted him to share that moment with me. I believe he got it wrong on that occasion. He made mistakes too; he was human.

There were many times I got it wrong as well. I was diagnosed with an underactive thyroid in the 1980s. I thought I was losing my mind, and suicidal thoughts were working on me. I would get mad at him in a heartbeat and carry on about something minor for hours! I called my sister who lived in Greenville, South Carolina, at that time, and asked her if I could come and stay with her for a while! I was ready to LEAVE him because he forgot to pray for my special prayer request one Sunday! It's funny now, but it wasn't funny then! Bill put up with me and suffered through it until I got a correct diagnosis and proper medication. My mind cleared up, and my personality came back to normal. Whew! That was rough on both of us, but I believe it was harder on Bill to watch me spin out of control without knowing what was wrong. I'm human also. We all are.

My beloved was the BEST lover, a wonderful singer, as funny as they come, faithful every single day, and many, many other things, but he could not close a door, turn off a light, or close a drawer. He could not put his dirty clothes in the hamper or clean the hairs off the sink when he trimmed his beard. You know…regular "guy" stuff.

He would be the first to tell you that my idiosyncrasies drove him CRAZY! I am a bit of a germaphobe. Bill was never afraid of a "stinkin' germ!" I didn't like to touch fruit that had a bad place on it, and Bill would eat something that looked rotten to me and say, "AH, it's alright, Woman!" Blake said his daddy would eat stuff that could walk right out of the refrigerator on its own! Expiration dates meant nothing to Bill! He would see something that came over on the Ark, give it a sniff, take a bite, and declare that it was "alright."

I drove him crazy, and he drove me crazy, and we loved each other with everything inside of us. We fought the good fight together — ALWAYS together.

Birthday card from Bill December 2013

Well, my love, you have caught up to me at 59. Life has so many "pulls" right now for us. I am indeed glad to have you. I love your hugs, your smiles, your kisses. I need them so much. I miss you and look forward to our date day on this, your birthday. How precious is your love for me!

Valentine card from Bill (no date)

Through all seasons our love prevails. I can't stop loving you.

FaceBook Post from Bill December 14, 2021

Happy Birthday to my precious wife. All of my adult years you have been my constant companion and loyal supporter. You love me and that makes my life full. Oh my, how glad I am that The Lord sent you to me.

Christmas 2021 (Note handwritten on a sheet of white paper)

Merry Christmas! I have been sick for too much of December. Did not get to do birthday or Christmas shopping done as much as I wanted. I sure did enjoy our birthday date at Red Lobster. I just love having you home and seeing the glow of the Christmas lights in your face. You are and have always been my very best Christmas gift. I love you so, Bill.

Love is not always passionate nights of love-making. It's not always roses and candlelit dinners. For me it was lying awake at night and making sure that Bill was breathing. Sometimes it was him rubbing my legs when I had a bad cramp at night or fixing me a healthy meal when I was down in the bed with my back. Love is sometimes spending nights in hospital rooms trying to sleep in those ridiculously hard recliners (chairs of suffering). Love is crying in each other's arms when disappointments and hard times break your hearts. Love is also remaining faithful when illness makes intimacy impossible and enduring bad moods, because sick people are often moody.

Love is a commitment. I remember waking up one morning in Franklin Springs before we had even been married for two years. Something Bill had said or done had made me angry, and I suddenly had a thought!

"I'm not AFRAID of you!"

Bill laughed whenever I told that story. He knew that I was never afraid of him; he would never, ever have done anything to physically hurt me. When folks start dating and falling for someone, there is a little bit of fear that we will do or say something that will cause them to break up with us. That's what hit me. I was mad at him, and I was no longer afraid that he would leave me. I also had another realization about that same time.

There were times when I did ***NOT LIKE*** Bill Jones! Gasp! Guess what else? There were times he did NOT like me either!

"Like" is fickle; it comes and goes. It's all emotions. True love is deeper; it is a commitment to someone that must mean more. It must.

I always gave my students this illustration.

Me: ***Do you love your mother?***

The answer was always, ***"Yes!"***

Me: ***Do you "like" her every day?***

Pause…thinking…thinking…

"Well, no, not every day."

A marriage is the same way. We must love our spouses every single day; the commitment must be sure, but we will ***NOT*** like them every single minute of every day. Somedays they will drive us out of our minds and make us truly angry. We have to be willing to STAY until we LIKE them again. I can assure you that you will if you give it time and fight the GOOD fight.

Bill and I suffered more than our share of disappointments and hard times. I can say to you in absolute honesty that I would not trade the fifty-one years I had with him for any amount of time with someone else and an easier path. I often told my female students that we all have dreams of a strong, bodice-ripping guy with defined abs like the drawings on the front of romance novels! What we truly NEED is a faithful man who will cook for us and make us laugh! Now that is a combination for happiness! I never doubted Bill's love for me; I never doubted his faithfulness. He protected me and took care of me; he spoiled me in many ways. He did the very best he could for me in spite of health challenges that would have destroyed many men. When I describe him as courageous —as a warrior— there is not one bit of exaggeration in those descriptions. Even when he became frail, even at his weakest, his spirit was strong!

Facebook Post from Karen on 40th Wedding Anniversary

I have watched my husband preach, teach, and lead with integrity, and I have always been proud to stand beside him! As many of you understand, there are tough times in the ministry. Bill serves the Lord with his whole heart. He has always been willing to tackle tough issues, and he has never backed down from what was right. I admire him for his willingness to reach out to people and love them in the hard places. I have seen him sacrifice his rest, his time, and his finances to help others. He is one of the best friends anyone could ever have.

> ***Thank you, Lord, for bringing us together. We have weathered some tough storms, and we have also witnessed many mighty miracles. It has been an honor and a privilege to be loved by this man for forty-two years, and to be his wife for forty. My life is richer because you are in it. I love you, Bill Jones!***

Do I wish that Bill had not suffered chronic illness? Of course! Do I wish that we could have enjoyed decades of passionate intimacy? Absolutely! Do I wish he had not been hooked up to c-pap and bi-pap machines at night? Do I wish he hadn't had to wear an insulin pump and a defibrillator? You betcha! Do I wish we could have spent our 60s traveling instead of him using a walker and a wheelchair and spent our 70s and 80s together? You know the answer already.

Even though Bill and I were the same age, had the same religious training, and attended the same college, we were distinct individuals. Bill was more emotional and demonstrative than I am. He told me EVERY SINGLE day that he loved me and that I was beautiful. I know that most women do not hear that every day, and I am very thankful. He was more of a "hugger" than I am. He was definitely the extrovert, and he worked for over fifty-two years to PUSH me out of my tendency to be an introvert. Bill also had a very tender heart, and he thought I was too cynical. I like to think of myself as cautious and reasoned rather than cynical. Bill would seek out my opinion on folks at times because he could be too trusting which made him a target for some folks. He told me often that God had placed us together to balance each other out; I agree. Bill would cry more easily than I ever did — until now. I have cried every single day since he died; tears come quite easily to me at this point.

I think I will choose to be thankful for the fifty-one years we shared when no one ever expected that to happen. I will praise God for the seventy years he gave Bill to this world. I will be proud when I think of the wonderful sermons he preached and the lives he impacted for eternity! I will rejoice when I remember the delightful laughter we shared together, the silly songs he sang to me, and the fabulous meals he cooked. I will thank God for his devotion to me and for the tender love and passion Bill showed me whenever he was healthy. I will be thankful that Blake had a wonderful daddy until he was twenty-nine years old. I will ***REJOICE*** in the **MIGHTY** miracles God performed on our behalf.

Writing this book has brought it all back to me in such a precious way.

I will say it again, if we hadn't lived this story, I would have a hard time believing it myself.

Chapter Twenty-nine

Goodbye for Now

Letter from Karen: June 26, 1973

You're the one and only for me. You're the only person I can picture spending the rest of my life with, having children with, growing old with. I just can't picture my ever being without you. I pray I never have to be without you.

Letter from Karen: July 2, 1973

You can never know the love that I have for you. I can't even understand it all myself. If anything would ever happen to you — I would lose my mind. I can't imagine life without you anymore.

Letter from Karen: August 7, 1973

My life is empty when you're not around. I need to be near you and feel your love. My goal in life is to serve God and to be a good and loving wife to you. I want you to always love me and need me. Never stop needing me; for as long as you need me, you'll love me, and I'll be there by your side for the rest of my life.

Letter from Karen: August 13, 1973

God brought you into my life, and I never knew that there was such a thing as love like we have for each other. Our marriage is going to be beautiful. I have no doubts. A love like ours isn't going to die or grow old. It will only grow as our marriage matures.

Letter from Karen: August 25, 1973

It may be selfish, but when the time comes, I'd like for us to die together because I couldn't bear life without you. I'd like to see Jesus with you there. God gave you to me, and I want to thank Him in person. Oh Billy, these aren't just empty words; they come from the depth of my heart and soul! Never doubt my love; it's all here for you.

My precious husband left this earth on July 5, 2025. I was with him when he passed, but I did not go with him. He just slipped away in a hospital hospice room. Those beautiful eyes of his were accepted by the Georgia eye bank, and my prayer is that they were used to restore sight and that the recipients see Jesus through them. That is what Bill would want more than anything.

During his hospital stay, Bill instructed me to go home each night. During most of our marriage I stayed with him whenever he was hospitalized. As we aged, arthritis took a toll on me. Bill had very few joint issues which was a blessing, and he was so good to take care of me whenever my back or knees decided to throw hissy fits! He said if I tried to sleep on the chair of suffering, I would be in pain for days. He wanted me to be strong for when he came home from the hospital. Until the very end, we kept hoping he would be able to turn things around and come home again.

By July 3, I knew things were taking a wrong turn.

Facebook Post from Karen: July 3, 2025

Your prayers are what we need most. Bill is fighting for his life. I am very tired. Blake is worried. I thank God He is holding us up right now. PLEASE pray that Bill will receive the care he needs. He told me yesterday that he doesn't want to "fall in the cracks." He needs much help right now. Your prayers sustain all three of us.

My heart is full. Thanks so much for loving us!

Facebook post from Karen: July 4, 2025

As I sit in this dark hospital room tonight, I am thanking God for every breath that Bill breathes. His breath is labored now, but I am grateful to hear him breathing, to be in this dark room breathing the same air with him.

> ***We have loved each other for almost 53 years and have been married for 51. Praise God! We have weathered some storms and climbed some mountaintops. We have laughed, and we have cried. No one else shares the memories we have together. My heart is breaking at the thought of losing him. I cannot imagine that loss. I do not know what "that" looks like.***
>
> ***This I KNOW! God is GOOD. God has BLESSED us and KEPT us, and He has NEVER abandoned us. Whatever our future holds, God is in control. He loves Bill Jones more than I ever could. I can trust His loving arms, and I know that Jesus is in this room with us tonight. We are not alone; we are not walking this path alone. What a GIFT we have as Christians!***
>
> ***Blessed is the Lord God Almighty! Thanks be to God, the giver of ALL good things! Thanks to the God of our salvation, our HOPE of ETERNAL LIFE!***

I did spend the night at the hospital on July 4. We both got very little sleep, and I could hear fireworks in the distance. It all seemed a bit unreal. I simply could not leave him. He struggled quite a bit to breathe, and they finally gave him some morphine around 2:00 in the morning. A nurse asked me if I understood what was meant if they offered him "comfort" meds. I told her that I thought I did. They also spoke to both of us about wishes for resuscitation if his heart stopped.

The morning of July 5th was met with devastating news. A doctor came by and confronted Bill with the message that they had nothing else to offer him. They told Bill that he was dying; they recommended the removal of his regular medications and offered comfort meds instead.

Bill was awake and alert; he understood what they were saying. Blake and I were there with him. Bill's brother, Floyd, and his niece, Debbie, had driven from North Carolina to see him, and they were there as well. It was such a heartbreaking moment for all of us. Blake asked the doctor about time, and the doctor mentioned that some people live for over twenty days, but that Bill's health issues would make it "sooner rather than later." For some reason, that seemed to me that we still had a few days. I don't know what I was thinking; I suppose it was because Bill had always beaten everything before.

Blake, Floyd, and Debbie all left the room to make phone calls. I sat on the bed beside Bill. He just seemed stunned. I tried not to cry; I was trying to be brave, but my voice broke.

> ***"I know where you are going, but I don't want you to go. I will be coming…"***

> Bill quietly responded, ***"Don't be long."***

I don't recall if we said anything else or not. I helped Bill FaceTime his sister and her family in North Carolina, my brother and niece in Virginia. Yubo was able to FaceTime Bill twice from China. Thank God for modern technology in times like this!

The plan was to relocate Bill to a hospice room on another floor in the hospital. Staff told us that it would take a couple of hours to make the move. I told Bill that I was going to run home and shower and pack some fresh clothes. I had not brushed my teeth or showered, and I wanted to be ready to stay with Bill for however long we had. I cannot tell you how much I have regretted that decision; it haunts me daily.

I will say that when I got home and got into the shower, I broke down. The tears flowed along with the water from the showerhead. I sobbed and sobbed; this just couldn't be happening. As much as we had faced together, this entire scenario seemed out of my realm of acceptance. I showered, dressed, and packed a few things as quickly as possible and hurried back to Bill's new room.

Sadly, he was in a state of distress by then. I had only been gone a couple of hours, but the change was significant. He was sweating and a bit restless. I got the hospice nurse to give him more medication which did seem to ease things for him. He drifted off to sleep and seemed peaceful.

A dear friend from church offered to stay with me that night. I didn't want to impose, but she felt that I should not be alone. I thought I would be there with Bill for several days, so I accepted her offer for this "first" night. We were sitting there beside his bed talking quietly as he slept. I got up a time or two to wipe his forehead and put a wet sponge on his mouth. My friend walked into the hallway around 8:30 leaving us alone.

> ***"Honey, you can run to Jesus. Blake and I will be okay; don't worry about us."***

I said that because I knew we were supposed to say that. I am not sure I meant it. I didn't want Bill to die! I didn't want to lose him. I think I still thought he would somehow pull out of it.

At 9:18 pm, I received a text from our good friend and the Bishop of the International Pentecostal Holiness Church, Dr. Doug Beacham.

> ***"The Lord has all of you in His hands. When the time comes, Bill will open his eyes in heaven, fully well."***

I had been watching Bill's pulse in his neck. A few minutes after I read that text, I looked up to check Bill's neck again. I didn't see his pulse. I got up and leaned down to feel his breath on my cheek. I didn't feel anything. My friend was watching me anxiously.

I looked at her and said, ***"I think he is gone."***

Bill had just slipped away. He was making FaceTime calls mid-day and breathed his last around 9:30 that night. How could that be? I thought we would have a few days or that he would turn it around somehow!

I cannot tell you the burning tears I have cried because I did not crawl into that bed beside him. I have always seen that in movies; you know —the scene where the husband or the wife is dying, and the surviving spouse crawls into the hospital bed beside him or her. During the MANY hospital stays with Bill, I never tried to crawl into the bed with him because he filled up the narrow hospital bed! His broad shoulders took the space, and he wasn't well enough to turn on his side. Even though I know that, I still wish I could have been lying beside him. I wasn't holding his hand as he left this world; I wasn't singing to him. We had worship music playing on the phone, but I could not find my voice to sing to him. I know he wanted that, and I still could not do it. My heart breaks over that. I believe he would have sung for me, but I am not sure he could have done it either. I have sung by the bedside of others many times, but with Bill — my husband, my other "half"—it was different.

I should have done it for him. I should have…should have…but I simply could not. Even though I have struggled greatly with my shortcomings on that fateful day, I have reminded myself that Bill never had to watch me suffer; he never had to stand by a hospital bed and watch me as I slipped away. He never had to spend one single night trying to sleep in the chair of suffering while I was the patient.

Please understand that I am not minimizing the suffering of the actual patient, but I am recognizing the emotional agony experienced by any loved one who WATCHES the suffering. It can be paralyzing at times. In my own heartache, I am realizing that if Bill had been in that hospital room where I was dying; he ***might*** have had trouble singing to me as well. His voice might have been choked with tears in the very same way. The fact that I will never know for sure how ***he*** would have reacted is one of the reasons I still fight guilt. He was so strong; he might have been able to hold my hand and sing as he had always done for others. I will never know.

I am thankful that Blake could say whatever he needed or wanted to say to his dad. I am grateful for the video calls we placed on that Saturday afternoon. God allowed us to do or say whatever needed to be done or said. I feel that I am the only one who fell short, and I continue to fight guilt over it. They told me in GriefShare sessions that regret and guilt are normal; they encouraged us to give ourselves grace, and I am trying. I know that Bill is not angry with me in Heaven; I'm just angry at myself. I am working on giving myself grace; it is a work in progress at this point.

If I had that last day to do over, I would NOT go home for a shower. I would have crawled into that bed (if possible) and held him close to me until he took that last breath. I would have tried to sing — even if it were through salty tears. I would have told him over and over again how much I loved him and what a good man he was. I would have whispered sweet words of love to him for as long as he was breathing. I would have… would have…

I can't go back. I can't do it over. The ***ONLY*** thing I can do is forgive myself. All we can ever do in this life is our best. I thought that is what I was doing. I was trying to remain strong. I was trying to be brave. I was trying to be prepared. I was putting one foot in front of the other — like I had ***always*** done before. The difference is that I always brought Bill home before.

This time, I went home **ALONE**.

Chapter Thirty

What a MAN!

Bill Jones was MY MAN, my person. He sang to me; he tickled me; he made me laugh like no one's business! He loved me completely; I wish everyone could know a love like ours. He told me I was beautiful every single day, no matter what I actually looked like. Until Bill got sick, he just had the most beautiful skin; he was darker than I was, and he tanned easily. I am extremely fair-skinned. I still laugh when I remember how many times he'd come into the bathroom when I was dressing, and exclaim,

> ***"Lawd have mercy! I done married me a WHITE, white woman!"***

He was just so funny! Whenever I got mad about something, he knew just what to say to get me tickled so that I could get over my "mad." Having a husband who can make you laugh is the BEST gift! Bill was just fun to be around! Things were always harder for me whenever Bill's health took away his laughter. If he could tease me, I knew he was going to be okay. If HE was okay, I knew that WE were okay.

Happy Days

He had such a good voice — speaking and singing! His voice could calm a troubled heart or bring joy in the midst of brokenness. I have heard him sing over the phone as he ministered to people — hundreds, maybe thousands of times! He rarely preached without breaking into song at some point; it was just WHO he was. His silly songs to me are just memories now, but they are precious beyond words. He gave almost everybody a nickname and often used made-up phrases or words that just made folks smile. Our church members delighted in his crazy words; they often showed up on the church sign! God just gave Bill an "extra helping" of personality!

Bishop Bill Preaching

He was a wonderful preacher! I'm so glad; I would have hated to listen to a ***bad*** one for fifty-one years! He did have the anointed mantles from both of his grandfathers; Pinkie would have loved being able to see his powerful preaching! I hope God allowed her to do that on occasion. Anyone who heard Bill preach knew that he was an anointed "singing preacher" if there ever was one! There are SO MANY things that Bill said over the years that have resonated with many. Here are just a few that stand out in my mind:

> The devil doesn't care WHAT you believe as long as you believe it will happen TOMORROW!
>
> We are just an assortment of mixed nuts and bolts!
>
> It's Time! It's Time! It's Past Time!
>
> There are NO throwaway people!
>
> What we celebrate IS what we get more of.
>
> We must be SOLID spiritual markers in a world of MOVING spiritual boundaries.
>
> More Better Gooder!
>
> Super-dyna-whoppin'
>
> Sin makes you STUPID!

Bill often said that his sermon, "Sin Makes You Stupid!" was the one that more of us remembered than any other. He may have been right! If you were blessed enough to hear that sermon, you will agree with me. It was a masterpiece! We were changed by that sermon —not because of Bill's theological finesse —but because Bill took the theological truth and preached it at a level we could all understand; we could relate! Bill's strong voice and anointed delivery made it a JOY to listen to him. He preached that particular sermon as a young man, and I surely wish I had a recording of it. It would do us all good to hear that sermon ONE MORE TIME!

Bill loved to hear me sing and encouraged me in everything I did. He was a great teacher and counselor. He didn't just preach sermons; he pastored and shepherded his congregations faithfully. He loved each one of them dearly, even if some did not always love him back. He had a true shepherd's heart; he saw people as Jesus saw them.

Letter from Bill: July 25, 1973

God has been so good to me. He has helped me so much. He has called me to preach and given me so many things to help me be a good one. For one thing, He has given me lots of ideas for sermons, (youth) programs, and He has given me several chances to preach. Plus, He's given me, you. Someone to love me and for me to love. No preacher can be better than his wife. With you as my wife — plus God helping me — I should be a pretty good pastor. Oh Baby, I love you so, so very much.

Letter from Karen: June 9, 1973

I'm so deeply in love with you that I cannot even comprehend it myself. I believe with all my heart that God wants us together as a team and has a plan for us…I know that someday, we'll get together for good…

I often felt that I was unworthy of Bill; I just couldn't measure up. Bill always encouraged me, and I have come to realize that we did make a pretty good team. We balanced each other, and I did always try my best to support him. God knew what He was doing when He chose us for each other! I was always proud of Bill, and he was always proud of me.

It gives me great comfort to know that we spent fifty-one years together doing our best to serve God and to make a difference in this world.

IPHC Website Tribute: July 9, 2025

IPHC mourns the passing of Rev. William Noyel "Bill" Jones, former Superintendent of the Georgia Conference (now known as LifePoint Ministries). Presiding Bishop A.D. Beacham, Jr. shared: "Rev. Bill Jones served Jesus and the IPHC with distinction. I had the joyful honor of working closely with him in the Georgia Conference and serving with him on the IPHC General Board of Administration and Council of Bishops. He was a real friend and, most especially, a true servant of our Lord Jesus Christ. He and his wife Karen and their family always demonstrated great faith and perseverance."

Bill wasn't a perfect man, but he was a GOOD man. I thank God that he loved ME for almost fifty-three years and cherished me as his wife for fifty-one. He handled our finances until the last year of his life. He took care of my car and any type of maintenance on the house — even if he didn't always do it as fast as I wanted him to. He was a man's man. He could fix just about anything, and he was hard-working when his health allowed. He spoiled me in many ways, and I know that I took some of that for granted because he had always done it. He loved to cook delicious meals for me, and he took such good care of me whenever I was sick. He was very protective of me, but he was never controlling, and I was free to blossom within his loving protection. He was never jealous; he trusted me, and he gave me "wings." A weaker man would have wilted under my independent spirit, and I would have lost respect for him. Bill and I disagreed frequently and would stand up to each other "nose-to-nose"! Neither of us liked to lose an argument, but somehow, we would eventually find common ground. At the end of the day, we each respected the other's strength.

He was the "answer" to all of my questions. He was the "keeper" of our history; he remembered everything! All I ever had to do was ask Bill. I knew that he would tell me what I needed to know. He would fix whatever was wrong; he would give me the right advice for any situation. He was the BEST snuggler! He would wrap those long arms around me and pull me to his broad chest, and everything was alright in the world. I always felt SAFE in his arms. He loved me; he watched out for me. Even during the last year of his life, if I took a nap in the bedroom, I would hear him coming with his walker to turn off the light or put a blanket over me. He waited up for me at night and checked on me if I didn't feel well. He loved to hear me laugh and comforted me when the tears came.

Bill Jones made me a better woman. He pushed me to go beyond my self-imposed limitations. He encouraged me to dream BIGGER and reach HIGHER than I would have on my own. He believed in me and taught me to believe in myself. He had no patience with me when I doubted myself, and he'd get angry when I put myself down. He had NO tolerance for THAT! He loved to hear me sing, and I will never forget hearing his ***"Sing it, Girl"*** from the congregation! His encouragement thrilled me to the core.

When we went back to Elberton to pastor after being away for seventeen years, I shared with Bill that I needed a way to connect with new church members who didn't know me. I was busy teaching at Athens Christian and could not attend all of the mid-week activities. We came up with the idea that I would share what we called "Teachable Moments" each Sunday before he preached. I would share for ten-fifteen minutes and usually sing a song as well. He knew that he didn't always have the energy to preach a long sermon, so he also wanted us to "tag-team" on Sundays to give him a bit of a break. He trusted me enough to share the pulpit with me, and he enjoyed what I shared. Bill knew that my heart had always been to be an asset to his ministry; we were a team in every way. I thank God that Bill could depend on me; it means more than words can say.

After Bill died, a dear church member remarked that her young granddaughter had said she wanted a man "just like Pastor Bill." She had watched Bill love me, and at her young age, she was already hoping for God to send her a man like that. What touched me deeply was that the "Bill" this young girl saw was very frail. He used a walker or a wheelchair; his skin was very damaged from years of immuno-suppressing medications; his hair was thin and wispy. She was looking BEYOND his outward appearance and seeing the heart of the man inside. She wasn't believing for a fairy tale prince; she was hoping for a warrior husband to be part of her life's journey. I pray she gets one!

My heart has also been touched by so many wonderful cards, phone calls, and visits from former students. Several of them attended Bill's funeral or watched it online. Teachers are often forgotten, but God has blessed me with such love by many of my students; they continue to bless me and strengthen me YEARS after they sat under my teaching. Teaching is much harder than the average person realizes, but the rewards are life-changing. I taught Blake Taylor many years ago, but he continues to message me just to make sure that I am alright. This particular message touched my heart deeply.

> ***I never met Bill, but Bill touched my life. One day in (my) 10th grade English class, my teacher spoke on how a man should treat a woman. At the time, it seemed more of a share for the ladies in the classroom, but little did I know how incorrect I would be. Now, closing in on 10 years later, I am married to the love of my life. My teacher shared with us the love that is shown by the way her husband treats her. When I met my now wife, I remembered vividly the conversation you had with us. How Bill treated you. At the time, what seemed like a message to the ladies on finding a man who treats you with love and respect, is one that I carry with me to this day. I know it has been some time and you have led many classes but that is one I will never forget, and I strive to treat my wife the way Bill treated you.***
>
> ***With all being said, I may have never met Bill, but he did indeed change my perspective on how a son of God should treat a woman.***

Our love story is not special because every day was a romantic picnic; it is special because we FOUGHT to stay together through the hard places. Please know that even during the good times — the times when we weren't in a hospital room, or when Bill wasn't too sick to be loving — we still had seasons when we struggled with the mundane. We fought over the everyday things that annoy every couple — finances, parenting, snoring, restaurant choices, and pretty much anything else you can think of. We got bored with each other at times; we fought temptations just like anyone else!

Here is a BIG shocker; sometimes we went to bed ANGRY! Please don't think that I recommend that; it is NOT a good thing, but I promised to be honest. I cried myself to sleep many nights because he was so incredibly stubborn, and I KNOW he was more than aggravated with me on many occasions. There were times when we both failed and missed the mark. It took quite a bit of compromise and forgiveness to keep us on track. Marriage is the toughest job anyone will ever have, but it is worth the GOOD fight. I don't want anyone to look at our story and see it through the soft lens of a romantic movie; I am fighting a bit of that in my own mind now as I relive our precious memories. It isn't fair to either of us if I create a dream story that isn't real. Our true love story deserves better; it deserves the truth.

In many ways our story is more of a WAR story! We never lost sight of the VALUE of our love, and we were willing to fight to maintain it. We fought to stay together; we fought to get through those seasons of DISLIKE and get back to seasons of LIKE. We fought to get through one health crisis after another with the ever-present hope of healthier days. We fought for the privilege of being parents. We fought for each other whenever we felt attacked from outside forces. Don't be afraid to fight the GOOD fight; it is ***GIVING UP*** that will destroy a marriage. Bill and I did have to fight too many battles, and I sincerely wish we had enjoyed an easier road together.

I have to give God praise when I look back and observe the journey He designed for that little girl from Natural Bridge, Virginia, and that little boy from Clinton, North Carolina. He gave us a love that survived the odds; He allowed us to meet some of God's most precious servants along the way; He opened doors for ministry on local levels and in denominational leadership that we could never have imagined, and He gave us opportunities to travel and see so much of this beautiful world we live in! It wasn't a journey that we expected, and it was incredibly difficult and heartbreaking at times, but what an amazing journey it was![1]

Lasting Love

I wish every woman could have a man "just like Pastor Bill." He was MY man. I wish EVERY man could BE a man like mine! He wasn't perfect, but neither was I. Don't waste

1 See Appendix B

time looking for someone perfect; he or she does not exist! When God sends you a good spouse who loves you, work hard at focusing on the good, and be willing to forgive the bad. Fighting FOR your marriage is the GOOD fight. We survived because we never gave up; our love was worth the fight. Love is ALWAYS worth the fight.

I am deeply thankful for the fifty-one years we shared together as man and wife, and no matter how many years we could have had together, it would never have been enough. Living life without Bill just wasn't an option for me, but here I am. My heart is broken, but I have to praise God for the life we had together. What a LOVE I have known! What a journey I have made!

What a journey ***WE*** made ***TOGETHER***!

Postscript

(Written November 11, 2025)

Facebook Post from Karen: June 12, 2015

On Monday, we will celebrate 41 years of marriage. During that time we have laughed until we cried, and we have clung to each other in tears of despair. We have faced the familiar and the unknown, and we have faced it together. Life has given us a few dents and dings along the way, but that's life. I praise God for LIFE, and I thank Him for the life He has given me with Bill Jones. It hasn't always been easy, but it has NEVER been boring! (SMILE) I am so grateful that we have been able to grow older together. For those of you who know our story, you realize what a wonderful miracle that is!

When Bill slipped away on July 5th, my friend left the hospice room to call her husband with the news. I was alone in the room. I cried for a moment; I bent down and kissed him on the forehead, and I began to praise God. It may seem strange to some, but I felt that I MUST fill that room with praise!

I've read many accounts of people who've had NDEs (Near Death Experiences), and a common occurrence is that the spirit leaves the body and observes what is happening. I wanted Bill to SEE me praising God in that room! I thanked God for such a good husband; I thanked Him for giving Bill to us for seventy years and for our fifty-one years of marriage! I praised God for His faithfulness to us and the many miracles He performed for us. Even in my brokenness, I had to give God the glory He deserved whether Bill could see it or not.

I truly felt that "bubble" of protection for that first week without Bill. Funeral arrangements were taken care of; phone calls were made. Food was brought to the house; family arrived from Virginia, North Carolina, and Florida. It was a whirlwind of activity. I spoke for a few minutes at Bill's service, and many were astounded that I could do that. I knew that Bill would want me to share. I can tell you that when I got up and stood behind the pulpit it was as if I were "outside myself." I knew that the Holy Spirit was holding me up; I knew it was a supernatural moment.

The impact of the loss hit me on Monday afternoon, July 14, about 2:00. The last of the family drove away, and Blake went back to work. I did okay for about two hours. I had gone to the bathroom, and when I started to wash my hands, I looked at the mirror. I don't know why that ignited the wave of grief, but it did. I began to weep, wail, scream, and even beat the countertop with my fists! This lasted for about two hours; it wore me completely out! I have never before experienced such a powerful wave of emotion in my life, but I know now that it had to happen. Grief MUST be expressed; it is a natural and necessary part of a great loss. Losing a spouse is a GREAT LOSS; it cannot be explained without experience, and ***NO ONE*** wants that experience.

Letter from Karen: July 22, 1973

...Never forget that I do love you, and that I want nothing more than to be your wife. I know that you love me; you make me feel proud of myself...you make me feel pretty, and most of all, you make me feel loved and wanted. I trust you, and I know that I'll be happy with you. I hope that when you come after me in September, that we'll never have to be separated for any long periods of time again.

I am still dealing with heavy grief. I don't really know who I am now — without Bill. Half of ME is gone. I spent my entire adult life leaning on Bill; now, I have to stand up on my own, and it is scary at times. I said that I hoped we would never again have to be separated for a long time, and now I am looking at the rest of my life without him. I don't know HOW to do that! Without the Lord, I would be completely lost.

I understand why some folks retreat from society after losing a spouse; some contemplate suicide. I get it. Facing life without Bill is the hardest thing I have ever done. I know God has left me here for a reason; I believe writing this book is one of those reasons.

I thank God for Blake. He has been grieving himself, but he has done a good job of watching after me. His daddy would be proud. God knew how much I would need Blake at this stage of my life, and I am grateful for his company and his help. Yubo has kept in touch and even got here for a visit a few months after Bill's death. He loved Bill and wanted so much to get back to America before Bill passed away. He simply could not arrange it. My boys (young men now) are helping to hold me up.

Karen and her boys

You have read much about our struggles, our heartaches, and our trials, but please know that we had some absolutely WONDERFUL times as well. Those years after his first transplant were just delightful! They are especially precious to me because he could enjoy loving me, and "love me" he did! I adored the man, and I delighted in his love; my heart had been crushed by abstinence I did not ask for. When God allowed us to enjoy intimacy again, it was glorious for both of us. I suppose you could say that those years were like a second honeymoon for us. What a blessing!

Things did become trickier after the second transplant, but Bill still had seasons of time when his health held steady. During our fifty-one years of marriage, we took many wonderful vacations together. We went to California more than once, saw the Grand Canyon multiple times, went to Niagara Falls, drove through Texas, went to Disney World, took a couple of cruises, and toured several Hawaiian Islands for our twentieth anniversary. We enjoyed date nights and dinners with friends, and we were always ready to go see a movie together! We enjoyed football games and school activities with Blake and then Yubo. Bill preached with anointing and traveled all over America and to many foreign countries. He loved

Bill in Scotland

for me to go with him when I could, and he always wanted me to sing. Those weekend trips to churches across Georgia were good ones. Since I was teaching full-time, they were tiring for me, but Bill did his best to make them enjoyable, and I am so happy for the friendships we made and the ministry we shared together. We always loved taking trips together! We were best friends as well as lovers, so we thoroughly enjoyed doing things ***together***. I was able to travel with him to Costa Rica for an IPHC conference, and it was a wonderful trip. He once went to Great Britain with me when I chaperoned a group of middle school students. Great memories for sure!

We ENJOYED life, and we enjoyed it TOGETHER! As hard as things were, we made the best of it. I do give Bill the credit for that. He refused to allow his medical conditions to take over his attitude. When he would get depressed and angry, I knew things were truly bad. Most of the time he just pushed through and enjoyed each day to the best of his ability. That enabled me to enjoy it as well. Laughter is GOOD for us; it can be the BEST medicine on the WORST day; please remember that.

This book was written to honor Bill Jones and his memory, to testify of the goodness of God and His miraculous works. This story needs to be shared, and I am the only one who can tell it now. One day I will join Bill in Heaven; I want this book to be around so that others will know our miraculous journey! We serve a LIVING God who still works miracles, and He will do the same for you.

What does the future hold for me now? I have no idea. This has become my prayer:

> ***Lord, hold my hand and lead me through this dark valley. Guide me because I don't know the way. Your will be done in my life; help me to hear Your voice and follow Your direction. You are my Bridegroom; fill the void left in my heart, and please give me the strength to keep going.***

God blessed me with the very best parents anyone could ever have. Whenever my daddy was with me, I felt completely safe. I might not know where I was going, but if Daddy was holding my hand, I could follow him without fear. I didn't need to know the destination because I KNEW that my daddy would never steer me wrong.

As I continue to walk on life's journey without my precious and beloved husband, I feel very much in the dark. Bill watched over me and protected me; he was always looking out for me. He always gave me good advice and pointed me in the right direction. My heavenly Father will do the same; I am holding his hand in the dark right now. I cannot see the future, and everything feels strange and frightening. God knows my destination; nothing has taken Him by surprise. He still has plans for me, and all I need to do — all I CAN do — is hold tightly to His hand and follow His lead.

He has taught me that He SEES me! He KNOWS every tear I have cried. He GAVE Bill to me; He BLESSED our marriage; He UNDERSTANDS my heartache and the depth of my loss. Most importantly, God LOVES me, and I can TRUST Him. How wonderful is that!

Facebook Post from Bill: June 15, 2017

I am so delighted to have my wife back home from a visit with her parents. She got home in time for us to celebrate our 43rd Wedding Anniversary today. I am looking forward to our date day together. Thank you, my love, for being my wife, my friend, my heart, for these 43 years. You are truly God's unique gift to me.

Facebook Post from Karen: June 15, 2018

Forty-four years ago, Bill and I began our married journey! We were only nineteen years old and had NO IDEA how tough this journey would be.

We were talking last night about what it takes to have a successful marriage. Young folks believe that LOVE is all they need! ...

Oh my! You need LOTS of forgiving, lots of compromising, lots of putting up with each other, and lots of patience and fortitude, BUT it is worth it to have a relationship that stands the test of time.

Facebook Post from Bill: June 15, 2019

45 years of love, 45 years of laughter. 45 years of watching for you in a crowd. Smiling when I finally see you. 45 years of hugs and kisses. Happy Anniversary, Karen Fitzgerald Jones. I hope God gives us many more.

Facebook Post from Bill: June 15, 2024

On this day fifty years ago Karen and I stood before Pastor Conald Fogus in Natural Bridge, Virginia, and vowed to love, honor, and cherish one another in sickness and in health. She did not know what a demanding promise that would be, but yet she loves me still. Happy Anniversary, Karen Fitzgerald Jones! I do love you so!

Joneses and Griffins 50th Anniversaries

We NEVER expected to reach our 50th anniversary, and we actually made it to our 51st! One of my precious former students gifted us a few days at a condo in Pigeon Forge to celebrate our 50th, and Billy and Paula were able to join us. Bill was using a walker by then, and we couldn't do a lot of sightseeing, but we did enjoy a great show and some good food while we were there. We also played games in the condo and laughed more than is legal! We are all thankful for that great time together.

Bill said that he was glad the Lord sent ME to HIM. Now that you know our story, you KNOW that God sent HIM to ME as well! God chose us for each other, and we had no doubts about that. How glad I am for that — grateful beyond words! As difficult as it was at times, I cannot thank God enough for choosing me for Bill and for causing Bill to SEE me that night in the Franklin Springs Church! Oh my! I cannot praise Him enough for allowing me to share nearly fifty-three years of my life with that man. It was an honor.

My hope is that you have laughed at our shenanigans and cried with us during our heartaches. I pray that you will be inspired by our story; that you will persevere in your own marriages. I pray that you will BELIEVE for miracles in your own life; we serve a God who is ABLE! Ask and keep on asking; don't give up on the miracles in your life.

I have learned that a life of struggle doesn't necessarily mean a life of sadness. We lived and loved; we laughed and cried; at times we failed, but we endured; we persevered, and we triumphed! It is worth the effort; I promise you! Do the hard things, and make every moment count. Love each other through the difficult places when you don't particularly ***like*** each other. Forgive freely and ***OFTEN***; it's not an easy thing to do, but it is necessary. Staying together is not only the ***RIGHT*** thing to do; it's the ***BEST*** thing to do. Growing old together is a divine gift; we never expected it, and we were so grateful for the privilege.

Compromise when necessary and keep saying, ***"I love you"*** as much as you can.

Bill would say, ***"Love makes everything SUPER-DYNA-WHOPPIN' and***

MORE BETTER GOODER!"

He was right; it does!

Acknowledgments

Ordinarily, Bill would be the first person I would thank in a situation like this. Even though he is no longer physically with me, I want to thank him for loving me, for asking me to be his wife and to share life's journey with him. Had he not accepted God's will for his life — which included ME — there would be no story. It is important to remember that God does not force things on us; we have free will. When Bill poured out his heart at the altar in Franklin Springs that cold January night in 1973, he had choices to make. He could have rejected the call to preach, and he could have resisted God's plan to include me. I am incredibly grateful that my dear husband accepted both that night!

Bill's sister, Evelyn (Blake) Jones McKenzie, and my nearly life-long best friend, Paula Price Griffin, deserve many thanks for their life-giving gifts of donated kidneys which extended Bill's life nearly 42 years! I almost lost him at the age of twenty-seven. Words are simply not enough to express what that means to me. Evelyn's and Paula's families must also be thanked for their willingness to support their decisions to donate one of their kidneys to Bill. What love they all showed; they are truly heroes in every sense of the word.

I want to thank Reba Rambo for obeying God when He prompted her to call me that beautiful February day in 1996! If she had resisted the urging of the Holy Spirit, we would never have had our son, Blake. She allowed Blake to be dedicated in California, the day after his birth, wearing a beautiful dedication gown handmade by Reba's mother, the renowned Dottie Rambo! Her loving kindness towards us during that miraculous time was truly extraordinary. What a treat for Reba to write the Forward to this book as well!

I thank my parents who loved me and gave me every opportunity to thrive in this life. They loved Bill as another son, and now Bill is rejoicing in Heaven with Mama by his side. Bill's mom and dad are there as well as his sister, Lib, and my sister, Sandy. Heaven is also populated with a stillborn brother I never met and more grandparents, aunts, uncles, and cousins than I can name here. My eternal destination looks sweeter every day as more and more of my loved ones wait for me there.

My son, Blake, and my Chinese son, Yubo, deserve many thanks for loving me and putting up with me at times! Of course, I might deserve an award for putting up with them, but that's the job of every mother in the world! I am just thrilled that God saw fit to give me the experience of motherhood and all that goes with it! I cannot fathom the depth of loneliness that I would experience now without my sons to support me.

I am very grateful for the input of those who read the first drafts of this book and offered their advice regarding corrections. No matter how many times I read over the drafts, I still missed things! What mattered even more to me was their input regarding the content. They were so encouraging; they kept me writing and revising! Kudos to Bill's sister, JoAnne Jones Logan; my brother, Barry Fitzgerald; my cousin, Ginny Turner; my sister-in-law, Sheila Jones; my bestie, Paula Price Griffin; and my friend and colleague, Tammy Sparks; they all sacrificed their time and put up with my pestering! Chris Maxwell, Dr. Doug Beacham, Dr. Andrea Daniel, and Rev. John Case also gave their time and energy to read a draft and offer their input and give their endorsements which I value highly. I also thank Sue Beitzel and Lara Gaines for reading over particular chapters for me and offering their respected advice.

Thanks to my publisher, Steve Spillman and True Potential Media. You have been a wonderful source of guidance for me on this new journey. You deserve an award for NOT losing patience with all of my questions! I am glad that Chris Maxwell pointed me in your direction. This has been a great experience for me!

To every church member, fellow pastor, and friend who supported our ministry over the years, I thank you. Thank you for standing with us when the attack was fierce. Thank you for stepping into unknown territory with us when it was uncomfortable. Thank you for praying for us during difficult seasons of life and ministry and rejoicing with us in the miraculous interventions. Thank you for allowing us to cry on your shoulders during the tough places. Thank you for coming by the hospital to see Bill during the MANY hospital stays he had to endure, for buying my lunch, and for slipping money into our pockets or our hands during your visits. Each kindness shown and each prayer prayed have been documented in Heaven and engraved on my heart forever. Bill and I could never have accomplished anything for the Kingdom without the love and support of so many over the years. Thank you for taking this life journey with us and holding up our arms when we were too weak to do it ourselves. God knows each of you by name; may He continue to richly bless you and supply every need!

Lastly, I will take a moment to thank Jesus for all He has done in my life. He is certainly NOT last place in my life, but I wanted to give Him a bit more space here. I gave Him my heart in a primary Sunday School class when I was eight or nine years old. I had not committed any gross sins at that point, but I recognized that I needed a Savior, and He changed my life forever at that moment. During every season — good and bad — of my life; He has been present. I have never met him face-to-face, but I FEEL His presence with me every single minute of every day. He has loved me in my best moments and in my worst. I have discovered that His love for me is stronger than any anger or pettiness I may express, and I have often expressed both. He has worked many miracles in my life, but there have also been prayers — sincere prayers- when His answer was either "No," or "Wait," and I haven't been happy with either of those. Writing this book has helped me to look at my past through a different lens, and I do see the hand of God much more clearly from this perspective. As I face an unknown future, it helps me to know that Jesus is by my side. I have so much evidence of His presence; I no longer question it during the dark times. I simply know that He is with me, and I trust Him to guide me through whatever comes my way. He will do the same for you; all you have to do is trust Him.

If you have read this book, and if you have not accepted Christ as your Savior, I pray that you will. He loves you more than anyone else ever could. He is FOR YOU. He will heal the brokenness, and He will give you a new path to follow. I plan to join my beloved Bill in Heaven one day; I KNOW that he is waiting there with so many of our loved ones. Jesus is also waiting there for me; He is the reason I have that HOPE of Heaven!

I would love for YOU to be there as well; I do not want anyone to miss Heaven. Nothing would thrill me more than to know that this book turned your heart toward Jesus! Nothing matters outside of Christ — NOTHING. Everything we work for in this world will someday just be dust. Bill used to say that one day we will all just be pictures on the wall in a Cracker Barrel somewhere! We would laugh at that, but there is much truth to it. We work so hard for STUFF that will one day just be taken to the local dump, thrifted, or sold in a yard sale. Let's work harder to make sure that our hearts are committed to Jesus. The only thing that will last in this life is what we do for Him.

If you want to accept Jesus Christ as your Savior, you only need to ***ask*** him. Prayer does not have to be fancy. When Jesus was crucified, one of the men being executed beside him simply asked to be "remembered" when Jesus entered His Kingdom. The man didn't pray a long prayer; he simply acknowledged that Jesus was Lord and humbly asked to be remembered. That was his way of asking Jesus to have mercy on him — a sinner. Don't allow your sins to keep you separated from God. Don't think that you have to get "clean" before you come to Christ. The Bible says that any goodness in us is like a filthy rag to God. We can never be CLEAN enough for God. When we accept Christ and ask for His forgiveness; the blood He shed on the cross covers our sin, and God no longer sees it! How wonderful is that? I know it doesn't make sense to us, but that's okay. We are mere humans; God understands, and that is all that matters.

Talk to Jesus as you would talk to me. Confess that you are a sinner (we all have sinned) and that you NEED a Savior. Ask Jesus to forgive you and to accept you; make room for Jesus in your heart. You may immediately become emotional, or you may not feel a thing. Either response is irrelevant. What matters is your commitment to Him. To help yourself grow in Christ, it is so important that you find a body of believers (church or small group) who teach the Bible. We all need accountability. Read the Bible and pray; it is the nourishment your spirit needs to grow!

Bill would agree with me that our miraculous journey means nothing unless it inspires others to look to Jesus, the author and finisher of our faith! I began this book with God, and I will end it with God. *EVERYTHING* begins and ends with God, and I give Him ALL the glory and ALL the honor. Praise His glorious name!

With my most sincere gratitude,
Karen Fitzgerald Jones
December 13, 2025

Appendix A

Medicine List for Bill

(This was a document that changed frequently. Once we bought a computer and printer, it was much easier to update as needed. Bill was able to manage his medications at home, but we ALWAYS carried copies of this with us to help doctors and nurses when needed. His daily medications were quite complicated for most of his adult life. I bought him a small rolling cart which sat beside his recliner. It contained all of these medications plus Tylenol and Tums which he needed frequently. He also always had a blood pressure cuff, a thermometer, and a fingertip oximeter for checking his blood oxygen levels.)

Aspirin	81 mg	Once per day	Bedtime
Atorvastatin	40 mg	Once per day	Breakfast
Carvedilol	12.5mg	Twice per day	Breakfast and Bedtime
Colchicine	.6 mg	Once per day	Breakfast
Eliquis	5 mg	Twice per day	Breakfast and Dinner
Entresto	24-26mg	Twice per day	Breakfast, Bedtime
Eplerenone	50 mg	Once per day	Breakfast
Famotidine	20 mg	Once per day	Bedtime
Farxiga	10 mg	Once per day	Breakfast
Fenofibrate	48 mg	Once per day	Breakfast

Insulin	U500	Administered by Pump	
Isosorb Mono ER 120 mg		Once per day	Breakfast
Nitroglycerin	.4 mg	As Needed	
Magnesium	400 mg	Twice per day	Breakfast and Bedtime
Metolazone	2.5 mg	As Needed	
Omeprazole	40 mg	Once per day	Breakfast
Potassium	40 meq	Twice per day	Breakfast and Bedtime
Prednisone	5 mg	Once per day	Breakfast
Probenecid	500 mg.	Once per day	Breakfast
Sensipar	30 mg.	Once per day	Breakfast
Sirolimus	.5 mg.	Once per day	Breakfast
Sotalol	40 mg.	Twice per day	Breakfast and Bedtime
Torsemide	40mg	Twice per day	Breakfast and Dinner
Verquvo	10mg	Once daily	Breakfast
Vitamin C	1000 mg	Once per day	Breakfast
Vitamin D-3	1000 IU	Once per day	Breakfast
Zinc	50 mg	Once per day	Breakfast

Appendix B

Biographical Information for Bishop Bill Jones

William Noyel (Bill) Jones was born in Clinton, North Carolina. He was the fifth child of the late Henry Floyd Jones and Pinkie Medford Jones. He was a namesake of both of his grandfathers. His paternal grandfather, William (Billy) Jones, was a leading layman who helped pioneer pentecostal churches in eastern North Carolina in the early twentieth century. His maternal grandfather, Rev. Noyel John (N.J.) Medford, pastored some of the notable Pentecostal Holiness Churches in the North Carolina Conference during its first four decades

Reared on a small farm at the edge of Clinton, Bill graduated with honors from Clinton High School in June 1972. That fall, he entered Emmanuel College in Franklin Springs, Georgia. The Emmanuel years were formative and life changing. In January of 1973, during a winter quarter revival, he accepted his call to preach. The first person to whom he confessed this call was a young coed from Natural Bridge, Virginia, named Karen Fitzgerald. Young Karen would become his bride in June 1974.

While a student at Emmanuel, Bill served as President of the Emmanuel Ministerial Fellowship. He led a weekly ministry to Alto Correctional Institute for youthful offenders for which he was given a service award by the Prison Chaplain, Rev. Robert Foye. During 1975 and 1976, while still a student, Bill served as Assistant Pastor of the Athens Pentecostal Holiness Church with Pastor Paul Hopkins. In 1982, Bill was named *Outstanding Alumnus of the Emmanuel College School of Ministries.*

Rev. Bill Jones served three pastorates spanning twenty-nine years. His first pastorate upon completion of Emmanuel College was the Griffin Pentecostal Holiness Church from 1976 to 1978. He then pastored the Elberton Pentecostal Holiness Church from 1978 to 1984. In the end of 1984, he pioneered The Lighthouse, a new Pentecostal Holiness Church in the Elberton/Northeast Georgia area. He pastored The Lighthouse until July 1998. During the years at The Lighthouse, the church grew to be among the largest in the conference and birthed a notable shelter ministry for Northeast Georgia called SafeHouse Ministries, Inc. For the pioneering work at The Lighthouse, the Rev. Jones was granted the *Bishop's Award for Distinguished Service to the Pentecostal Holiness Church* in 1985.

Stricken with kidney failure in January 1982, the Rev. Jones survived hemodialysis for seventeen months until he was given the gift of life in the form of a donated kidney from his sister, Evelyn, in May 1983. This event in Rev. Jones's life served as a refiring time for his zeal for ministry.

Toward the end of their years in Elberton, the Joneses were blessed with the birth of a long-awaited son, Blake Jones. Reba Rambo had prophesied about this child five years before the miraculous birth took place in California. She remarked that "God moved heaven and earth for the Joneses to have Blake." Bill and Karen gratefully concur.

In June 1998, The Georgia Conference of the Pentecostal Holiness Church in its business session created a full-time staff position. Superintendent A. D. Beacham confirmed with the Conference Board that the new position would be in the areas of Evangelism, Missions, and Church Planting. Rev. Bill Jones was appointed to the position. The Rev. Jones was also elected in 1994 and reelected in 1998 to serve as Assistant Superintendent of the Georgia Conference of the International Pentecostal Holiness Church.

In August 2001, Rev. Bill Jones became the Superintendent of the Georgia Conference of the International Pentecostal Holiness Church when Dr. Doug Beacham was elected to be the Church Education Ministries Director for the denomination. In June 2002, the Georgia Conference in session showed great faith by electing the Rev. Jones to his first full term as Georgia Conference Superintendent though he was very ill with kidney failure.

On July 10, 2002, Bishop Bill Jones received a second kidney transplant from Paula Price Griffin, the close friend of his wife Karen Jones since their childhood. Yet again, with a gracious second gift of life, Bishop Jones moved with boldness into his first four-year term as Conference Superintendent and then in 2006 he was elected by acclamation for a second term as Conference Superintendent for Georgia. Bishop Jones was elected — once more by acclamation — in 2010 to serve his last four-year term as conference superintendent. He served the good people of Georgia for fourteen years (2001-2015) in this position as conference superintendent.

He returned to Elberton in 2015 to pastor once again. His former congregation, The Lighthouse, had been renamed Celebration Outreach Center during his absence. He pastored until 2022 when health issues caused him to pass the mantle to Rev. John Case. Rev. Case grew up in The Lighthouse and under the ministry of Bishop Jones. The church continues to honor Bishop Jones as the founding pastor.

Bishop Jones's contributions to the IPHC were many. On September 14, 2024, he was honored for fifty years of service as a minister in LifePoint Ministries (Georgia Conference IPHC). He served the denomination in many different areas over those fifty years. He pastored three churches; he also served on the General Board of Administration for the International Pentecostal Holiness Church. He served as Vice Chair of the Planning and Budgetary Committee for the denomination. He was a member of the Board of Trustees for Emmanuel College (now Emmanuel University) of which he served on the Executive Committee for the Board and Chairman of the Enrollment Management Committee. Bishop Jones also served on the Board of Trustees for Falcon Children's Home in Falcon, North Carolina. Bishop Bill Jones faithfully served with excellence wherever God planted him.

God called him home on July 5, 2025. After a life of devoted service to the Kingdom of God, he received his heavenly reward.

About the Author

Karen Fitzgerald Jones grew up in Natural Bridge, Virginia, but has spent most of her life in Georgia. She earned her A.A in General Education from Emmanuel College (now Emmanuel University), her B.A. in English Education from Tift College (now part of Mercer University), and her M.A. in English Education from Piedmont University.

At her core, Karen is a teacher. She taught seventh grade - college in both public and private schools for forty years before retiring to become a caregiver to her beloved husband. She taught pre-teens and teens in church classes for decades. She often shared "Teachable Moments" on Sunday mornings as she ministered alongside her husband. She has enjoyed speaking and singing at numerous churches, conferences, and retreats over the years. It's in her DNA, and she loves for her audience to enjoy the lessons!

She is in a new season now, and she is anticipating new opportunities for ministry. This is her first book, but she doesn't believe it will be her last. Karen relates to people because she is honest and down-to-earth.

She holds nothing back whether she is writing, singing, or sharing in a small group or a large crowd. Her life hasn't been easy, but God has been a constant presence through it all. People often describe her as "real." That's her heart – to be real and to encourage others to persevere and to keep believing!

> ***I cannot say my faith has been unwavering. I have always known God could answer my prayers; I simply doubted that He would. I know now that God's love is bigger than both my doubts and my anger! He has loved me enough to see me through tremendous difficulties. This is the God I serve. When people hear my testimony, they are able to look above and find hope for their own situations.***
>
> ***Karen***

Contact Information:

E-mail: middlejones@yahoo.com

Facebook: kfjones54

www.ingramcontent.com/pod-product-compliance
Lightning Source LLC
LaVergne TN
LVHW020712110826
845149LV00012B/2230